ISO 9001 AND
SOFTWARE QUALITY ASSURANCE

THE McGRAW-HILL
INTERNATIONAL SOFTWARE QUALITY ASSURANCE SERIES

Consulting Editor

Professor D. Ince
The Open University

Other titles in this series

Practical Implementation of Software Metrics – Goodman
Software Testing – Roper
Software Metrics for Product Assessment – Bache and Bazzana
An Introduction to Software Quality Assurance and its Implementation – Ince

Related titles on software engineering are published in an accompanying
series: **The International Software Engineering Series**, also edited by
Professor Darrel Ince.

ISO 9001
AND SOFTWARE
QUALITY ASSURANCE

Darrel Ince

McGRAW-HILL BOOK COMPANY

London · New York · St Louis · San Francisco · Auckland
Bogotá · Caracas · Lisbon · Madrid · Mexico
Milan · Montreal · New Delhi · Panama · Paris · San Juan
São Paulo · Singapore · Sydney · Tokyo · Toronto

Published by
McGRAW-HILL Book Company Europe
SHOPPENHANGERS ROAD · MAIDENHEAD · BERKSHIRE · SL6 2QL · ENGLAND
TELEPHONE 0628 23432
FAX: 0628 770224

British Library Cataloguing in Publication Data

Ince, Darrel
  ISO 9001 and Software Quality Assurance.
  – (McGraw-Hill International Software
  Quality Assurance Series)
  I. Title   II. Series
  005.3

  ISBN 0-07-707885-3

Library of Congress Cataloging-in-Publication Data

Ince, D. (Darrel)
    ISO 9001 and software quality assurance/Darrel Ince.
      p.   cm. — (The McGraw-Hill international software quality
  assurance series)
    Includes index.
    ISBN 0-07-707885-3
    1. Computer software — Quality control.   2. Quality control —
  Standards.   I. Title.   II. Series.
  QA76.76.Q351533   1994
  005.1′068′5 — dc20   93-48259
                                                           CIP

1234CUP97654

Typeset by the author
and printed and bound in Great Britain at the University Press, Cambridge

CONTENTS

ACKNOWLEDGEMENTS

Extracts from ISO 9001 are reproduced with the permission of BSI. Complete copies can be obtained by post from BSI Sales, Linford Wood, Milton Keynes, MK14 6LE.

QUALITY FORUM

The Quality Forum is pleased to publish jointly with McGraw-Hill this book which covers topics pertinent to software quality assurance.

The aim of the organization is 'to help the member organizations improve the quality of their products and services through the exchange of information between members and with other organizations with similar interests'.

The Quality Forum has over 200 members, including organizations from all sectors of industry and commerce, as well as local and national government. While these organizations are predominantly based in the UK, this includes a growing number from other countries in Europe.

This series of books aims to provide an opportunity for authors to publish works which are both practical and state-of-the-art. In this way Quality Forum members and other organizations will benefit from the exchange of information and the development of new ideas which will further the cause of quality in Information Technology.

The Quality Forum publishes these books with the aim of stimulating discussion in the software community so that the industry as a whole will move forward to improved products and services. It is proud to be associated with the series while not endorsing every single point of view in every book.

If you would like to know more about the Quality Forum, please contact:

Quality Forum
17 St Catherine's Rd
Ruislip
Middlesex HA4 7RX
UK
Tel: +44 (0) 895 635222
Fax: +44 (0) 895 679178

1

SOFTWARE QUALITY AND QUALITY ASSURANCE

1.1 INTRODUCTION

This book is about the ISO 9001 quality standard and in particular about its application to software development. The last five years have seen a rapid increase in the number of developers worldwide who are adopting the standard. Each of the remaining chapters of the book examines one particular facet of the standard. This chapter describes the meaning of the term 'quality' and its application to software products. It is a key chapter: it describes how software quality can be split up into a number of quality factors—sometimes known as quality attributes—and how a quality system is able to enforce various levels of these factors.

1.2 THE MEANING OF QUALITY

If you look at many of the books that have already been published on quality assurance you will see that they generally agree on what quality means. Usually their agreement is enshrined in the phrase 'fitness for purpose'. That is, a quality product—be it a car, refrigerator, hair drier or any other artefact—is one which does what the customer expects it to do. Fitness for purpose is an important concept, and forms a central tenet of quality assurance. Later in this chapter you will see that it is not the only property of a quality product. However, before examining the full story it is worthwhile examining a particular implication of the phrase 'fitness for purpose'.

The phrase implies that somewhere there will be a description of the purpose which an artefact is intended to carry out. For very simple artefacts this description might mainly be contained in the title of the artefact. For example, the term 'hair dryer' conveys the vast majority of the functionality of a device used to dry hair which is wet. For some artefacts the description of its purpose might be contained in a user manual which, as well as providing details about how to use the artefact, might include some technical specification. For large artefacts—for example, software or hardware systems—the purpose is usually enshrined in a document usually referred to as the *requirements specification*, sometimes known as the *system specification*. In reading this chapter all you need know about a requirements specification is that it contains a description of what a software system is to do, together with descriptions of constraints such as response time which are to be associated with the system. The requirements specification is the most important document generated in a software project; it is around this document that a quality system revolves.

The modern view of quality assurance takes a more sophisticated view than that of fitness for purpose. A high quality product is one which has associated with it a number of quality factors. These could be described in the requirements specification; they could be cultural, in that they are normally associated with the artefact through familiarity of use and through the shared experience of users; or they could be quality factors which the developer regards as important, but which are not considered by the customer and hence not included in the requirements specification.

It is instructive to examine some examples of each of these three categories of quality factors. The first category is those which would be contained in the requirements specification. An example of such a quality factor is *portability*. A customer for a software system may require that a system be executable across a diverse range of hardware architectures. Consequently, these architectures would be described in the requirements specification.

An example of the second category of quality factor, those which are cultural, is *usability*. Because a customer may have experience of systems in which it is relatively easy to communicate with a computer, he or she may not specify how an interface is to be implemented in detail in a requirements specification; there may be a brief directive to use a WIMP interface or a line-by-line command interface, but because of the same shared assumptions with the developer, the details of the interface would normally be omitted from the requirements specification.

The third category of quality factor is those quality factors which may be of interest to the developer, but not of direct interest to the customer. An example of such a quality factor might be *reusability*: the ability to transfer modules constructed for one software system into another software system. For example, a software developer may be currently constructing a software system for one customer which is somewhat similar to a system that he or she hopes to construct for another customer. If the second system is being bid for by a number of software developers, then the producer of the first system could gain a major commercial advantage during the bidding process by ensuring that the first software system is highly reusable. This advantage would, of course, be obtained by making a very low bid, since little new programming would be required. This category of quality factor is, at best, only of indirect interest to the customer, and would not be contained in a requirements specification. However, in the case of reusability a customer, while not perhaps asking for reusability in the requirements specification, may be interested in receiving a licence fee for the software that is reused.

It is important to point out that the three categories of quality factor do not represent a hard and fast taxonomy. What category a quality factor is placed in really depends on the customer, the customer's circumstances, the application area and the developer's circumstances. For example, I described usability as a cultural quality factor in that everybody expects their systems to be usable. Normally this is so in a large number of software systems. However, there are categories of software systems used for safety-critical applications where usability is of such importance that it is included in the requirements specification, for example by specifying a metric which quantifies the unacceptable frequency of erroneous commands being initiated by the operators of the system.

Even though the three categories of quality factor are not hard and fast, what is important is for a quality system to recognize that they exist, and to ensure that, right at the start of the project, the manager of the project examines all the quality factors that may be necessary before deciding on the quality controls that are required for a project. A project manager should not just assume that 'fitness for purpose' as exemplified in a requirements specification is enough.

It is now worth examining some of the important quality factors. The first quality factor is *correctness*. That is, that a software system actually conforms to its requirements specification; naturally, this quality factor should be totally present in any system.

The next quality factor is *maintainability* or *modifiability*. This describes the ease with which a software system can be changed. Originally change occurred with software systems due to errors being found by the customer. However, over the last decade or so it has become quite evident that many other categories of change occur. There are, of course, changes due to errors being committed—these will always be with us, although I would hope that, as technology improves, the extent of this category of change will lessen. There are also changes due to requirements volatility. Paradoxically, one of the indicators that a software developer has that a good system has been developed is to receive numerous requests from a customer for modifications which arise from changes in requirements. Often these are framed in terms of new functions.

Also, the developer will receive requests for changes due to a customer's external circumstances changing. For example, an accounting package may have been delivered which, although it satisfied the original customer's requirements, now has to be modified because tax laws have changed. Thus, nowadays, because customers demand more and more from successful systems, and external circumstances change, a high level of modification can be attributed to changes in requirements. There is another category of change: this is the set of changes which somehow improve a system without changing its functionality; tuning a system in order to give it a faster response time or rewriting a device handler to cope with a new output device are examples of such changes.

The first category of modifications—those due to error fixing—is known as *corrective changes*, the second category due to the developer responding to changes in requirements is known as *adaptive changes*, and the third category of changes which improve a system is known as *perfective changes*.

What is important is not the categories of change, but the fact that many software systems have a very high level of maintenance due to these changes, with the majority of the changes being adaptive. Moreover, many of these changes will not only occur during maintenance but, for projects which have a long time duration, will occur during the project itself. It is for this reason alone that I would say that the maintainability quality factor should always be present to a very great extent in every software system. After correctness, I would regard it as the next most important quality factor.

Maintainability is one of those quality factors which is normally only of indirect interest to the customer. Very few customers indeed include directives about maintainability in the directions they give a software developer, apart, of course, from those developers who intend to carry out the maintenance of a system themselves. However, it is worth pointing out that there will be an indirect interest in that software developers who build maintainability into their systems have a much greater chance of delivering a correct system within time and within budget. For example, if changes to a system are going to take a long time to apply, then there is always the possibility that when a high level of errors are discovered the duration of the project will increase past the estimated delivery time for the software.

Another quality factor which has already been mentioned previously is *portability*. This is the effort required to transfer a system from one hardware platform to another. Normally portability will be detailed in a requirements specification. However, for commercial reasons it is sometimes a quality factor that is of interest to the developer and only of indirect interest to the customer; as in the example cited earlier where portability was built into a system in order to give the customer a competitive edge during the process of tendering for another system.

Testability is another quality factor which is of direct interest to the developer, but is very rarely directly specified by the customer. It describes the ease with which a system, or part of a system, can be tested; for example, a system which has a very poor requirements specification containing a large amount of ambiguities and platitudes is very difficult to test, because the staff charged with system testing will have major problems in specifying the tests that check out the requirements specification.

Another important quality factor is *usability*. This is the effort required to learn, operate and interrupt a functioning system. Usability is often a major problem with systems: many software developers tend to think solely about the functions of a system at the front-end of a project, and then only bolt on an inadequate interface in the dying stages of the project. If anyone asks me to justify my obsession with quality factors and my contention that 'fitness for purpose' is not a wholly adequate basis for quality assurance, then I give them the example of the system which, when implemented, satisfies all the functions in its requirements specification but, because of a very poor interface, is grossly unusable.

Another important quality factor is *reliability*. This describes the ability of a software system to carry on executing with little interruption to its functioning. This quality factor is normally expected to be totally present in certain classes of safety-critical systems, and will often be specified in terms of metrics involving factors such as mean time between failure. For other types of system this quality factor will be cultural in that it will not usually be specified in a requirements specification, but will be assumed by the customer to be present to a high degree in a system.

Efficiency is another important quality factor. It is used to describe the degree to which computing resources, that is, file-space, memory and processor time, are used in an application. This is a difficult quality factor to categorize: many requirements specifications will contain detailed descriptions of the amount of hardware available and the desired response time. However, I would say that there are features which make it cultural in that a customer will expect, but not explicitly specify, that a software developer will make efficient use of the computing resources available to him or her.

Integrity is another important quality factor. This term is used to describe the extent to which the system and its data are immune to access by unauthorized customers. Again, this is a quality factor which cannot be precisely categorized: some systems, for example those used in financial applications, will have requirements specifications which describe the level of access allowed to such systems. However, there is often a cultural assumption that a delivered system should not be capable of being tampered with by unauthorized users or intruders.

Reusability is also a quality factor which is becoming increasingly important. It describes the ease with which chunks of software in one system can be moved to another system. This is normally a quality factor which is only of indirect interest to a customer.

The final quality factor which I will describe is *interoperability*. This is the ability of a system to operate in conjunction with another software system, for example a spreadsheet. Normally this is a quality factor which is specified in a requirements specification and is only of direct interest to a customer.

This, then, is a brief discussion of what a quality factor is. Many of you might have been tempted to regard it as somewhat academic; indeed, it is something of an academic game to derive longer and longer lists of quality factors.

However, there is a very practical reason for discussing quality factors this early in the book. It is connected with the fact that a quality system should be flexible. Normally, a quality system is embodied in a document known as a *quality manual*. At the beginning of a software project a project manager should decide which elements of the quality manual should be used to ensure the quality of the software that is to be delivered. In order to do this the quality manager should: examine a list of quality factors; identify those parts of the quality system which should be used to enforce the level of quality factor required; identify those parts of the quality system which should not be used; or even develop some new quality controls which may not be in the quality manual. A consideration of the quality factors to be built into a system, and the level to which they are to be built in, is often embodied in a checklist. Consideration of this checklist by a project manager at the beginning of a project drives the process of selecting quality factors.

Obviously there will always be components of a quality system which will be used in every software project, for example a standard for the requirements specification will always be needed; however, depending on the customer, application or software technology to be used, the project manager will decide what components of a quality system will be either used, strengthened or omitted. In order to understand this link between quality factors and the quality system it is worth examining some examples.

The first example concerns a system which is to be developed where the developer decides that reusability will be high in the system. This decision would normally be made by the manager of a project during the process of examining a quality factor checklist which contains a list of questions relevant to the particular factor. When the quality factor heading for reusability is encountered by the project manager there will be a number of questions which will drive the manager's thinking about that factor. For reusability there will be questions such as:

- Are we thinking of developing a similar software system in the future?
- Does our company have a policy of developing a reusable library of components?
- Are we currently bidding for a software system which has similarities to the one which is to be developed?

Let us suppose that the answer to the third question is yes, and the project manager decides to use a programming language such as C^{++} which has a high degree of reusability. A consequence of this might be that the quality system does not contain a programming standard for C^{++} and one has be developed; or an existing programming standard for C has to be modified since C^{++} is based on it.

Another example involves the development of a safety-critical system. Now such systems have to have massively high correctness and reliability quality factors. On examining the quality manual prior to starting such a project, the manager may decide that because this quality factor is so high then every technique for ensuring correctness which is contained in the quality manual has to be used. This armoury of validation techniques may be much larger than those which the project manager would normally deploy on a project for which the correctness quality factor was lower, for example a system for a clerical application.

A third example might be where a transaction-based system is to be produced for a customer who employs keyboard operators in an area of the country where such staff are in short supply. The project manager may decide—either after reading documents provided by the customer or in conversation with the customer—that a high degree of usability is required. This would mean that some usability studies would need to be carried out and usability testing would need to be scheduled during the later stages of the software project. The quality manual would be consulted and any sections pertaining to usability would have to be taken on board the project or, if non-existent, then they would have to be developed.

Thus quality factors, or more correctly a consideration of quality factors, forms the basis for the quality controls that are going to be applied in a software project. These quality controls are diverse and range from the application of standards to the application of tools. The following section describes them in a little more detail.

1.3 QUALITY AND THE QUALITY SYSTEM

The idea that the quality system should be flexible leads naturally on to a description of how quality systems work. The aim of this section is to describe the relationship that a quality system has with software development, and give the reader a vocabulary which will ensure that the remainder of the book can be accessed properly. At the heart of the application of quality assurance there is something called a *quality system* or, as it is increasingly known, a *quality management system*. This consists of the managerial structure, responsibilities, activities, capabilities and resources that ensure that software products produced by projects will have the desired quality factors that both the customer and the developer decide will be built into them. This means that a quality system encompasses activities such as:

- The auditing of projects to ensure that quality controls are being adhered to.
- The review of the quality system in order to improve it.
- Staff development of personnel employed within the quality assurance area.
- The negotiation of resources which enables staff who carry out quality assurance activities to function properly.
- Providing input into development-oriented improvement activities; for example, the adoption of a new notation for requirements specification.
- The development of standards, procedures and guidelines.

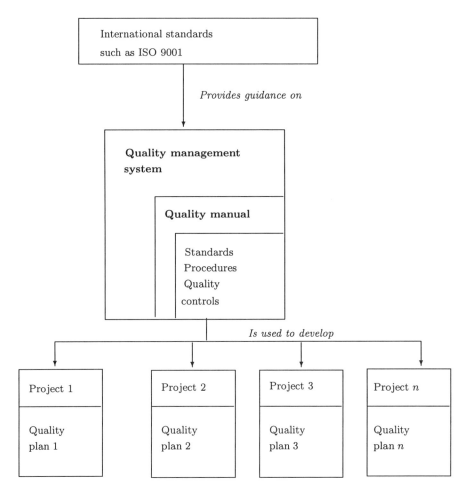

Figure 1.1 External standards, a quality management system and quality plans.

- The production of reports to high-level management which describe the effectiveness of the current quality management system.
- The production of reports to high-level quality management which enables them to put into action activities that result in the quality system being improved.

These, then, are a selection of activities normally associated with a quality management system.

The concrete details of a quality management system will be held in a *quality manual*—sometimes erroneously called a quality system. Such a manual will normally contain standards for the quality and developmental activities that may be applied to a project together with detailed descriptions of quality controls. The relationship between international standards, the quality management system and individual projects is shown in Figure 1.1. International standards such as ISO 9001 provide guidance to companies on how they should organize their quality management system. A component of the quality management system is the quality manual which describes the variety of standards and quality controls available to projects. When a project is in its formative stages—normally during planning—a project manager will identify the quality factors that are important, and extract out of the quality manual those standards and procedures which are necessary to ensure that the software product that is to be developed will contain those factors. He or she will also decide on the quality controls that are needed. These are placed in a document known as a *quality plan* which forms part of the overall project plan for a software project. A major part of the quality plan will describe how the quality controls are to be carried out, who will apply them, when they will be applied and other information such as whether special-purpose tools are required.

Thus, international standards such as ISO 9001 often—not always—drive the production of a quality management system. This then provides facilities for a project manager to produce a quality plan—there being separate quality plans for each project undertaken by a software developer.

As an example of part of this process consider a software project whose manager decides that portability is to be a major quality factor for a particular product. The manager will consult the quality manual for those parts which address portability and incorporate them as quality controls in his or her project. There are a number of ways in which the quality manual can provide facilities for ensuring portability, for example by providing standards for:

- The programming language chosen for the project which ensures that non-standard features are not used by programming staff.
- Portability testing across a wide range of computers and operating systems.
- Checking the output from any one-off or proprietary tools which process program code and detect non-portable features.
- Development techniques such as information hiding which enable a high degree of portability to be achieved.

A quality plan will embody a number of *quality controls* which check that particular quality factors are present in a system. A quality control is normally associated with documentary evidence that the quality factor is present. Some examples of quality controls are:

- An acceptance test which checks that a particular function has been properly executed. The documentary evidence would be a test record. This checks for correctness.
- The code review which, as part of its agenda, has been asked to check for portability concerns. The signed minutes of such a review would be the documentary evidence. This checks for portability.
- The execution of a tool which checks program code for adherence to programming standards. The printout from the tool indicating the absence of standards violations would be the documentary evidence. This enforces both maintainability and correctness since programming standards are developed to minimize errors when reading the code.
- The examination and signing-off of a test report by a senior programmer, the test report having been completed by a programmer who has just tested a number of modules in a system.

1.4 STANDARDS AND PROCEDURES

In order to finish this chapter, and to complete the process of providing a vocabulary, this section briefly describes the major tools provided in a quality manual: standards, procedures and guidelines.

First, a warning: paradoxically, for such an exact subject as quality assurance, nomenclature is still quite loose. The definitions that I give are accepted by a large number of software developers, but by no means the majority. I shall define a *standard* as an instruction about how a document should be laid out on paper or on a computer screen. For example, a requirements specification standard would specify all the sections expected in such a document and how each section is to be structured.

I shall define a *procedure* as text which describes how a particular software task is to be carried out. For example, a procedure for programming would describe what standards to apply, where to store the source code and object code of a program or module, how to carry out certain categories of test and what documentation to fill in when the process of programming and testing have been completed. The important point about both procedures and standards is that once they have been adopted for a particular project they have to be adhered to.

A *guideline* is text which provides advice on an activity. It is not prescriptive like a standard or a procedure. For example, a company may have a guideline governing the conduct of a project progress meeting which specifies who should normally attend such meetings. Although guidelines offer advice you would expect them to be adhered to by projects most of the time. Often, procedures and guidelines are found combined, where a procedure will mainly contain mandatory instructions but also provide advice, for example about how many staff should attend a particular meeting. The important point about such a combined document is that it should be made clear what exactly is mandatory and what is advice.

This section, then, provides you with a vocabulary. Before concluding, it is worth pointing out that companies sometimes refer to standards and procedures collectively as standards and sometimes as guidelines.

1.5 TECHNICAL ACTIVITIES

The aim of this brief section is to provide you with a vocabulary of technical terms. In the remaining chapters of the book I will be constantly referring to technical activities and this section briefly describes what they consist of.

Requirements analysis is the process of discovering the requirements that the customer has for a system. These requirements will be functional in that they will describe what the system is to do, or non-functional in that they constrain some aspect of a system such as its response time.

Requirements specification is the process of detailing the properties of a system which have been discovered from requirements analysis. These are embodied in a document which is often called the *system specification* or *requirements specification*. It is this document that forms the basis for all the subsequent developmental activities.

System design is the process of specifying the gross architecture of a system in terms of chunks of software which I shall refer to as *modules*. These chunks will be subroutines in third-generation languages such as FORTRAN and COBOL, or programmes in fourth-generation languages. A system design has to implement the functional properties of a system and, at the same time, respect the non-functional properties such as file size. These properties can be found in the requirements specification.

Detailed design is the process of specifying the individual modules in a system. Often this is done using a program design language which looks a little like a programming language or a flowchart-based notation. Many software developers omit the detailed design process and move directly to programming. *Programming* is the process of taking a system design or a detailed design and transforming it into program code.

There are a number of developmental activities which are aimed at checking out a system. The first is *acceptance testing*. This is the final test of a system which is carried out by the customer in the environment where the system will eventually be embedded. The acceptance tests check that the requirements specification has been correctly implemented. This is normally preceded by *system testing*. This is a series of tests carried out in the developer's premises which provide a high degree of confidence that the acceptance testing process will be successful.

Module testing, sometimes known as *unit testing*, is the process of checking out the individual modules of a system. Usually test data is selected which checks that a module does what the system design states it should do. Another important form of testing which, sadly, is often omitted by developers is *integration testing*. This is the process of building up a system adding a few modules at a time and then testing that the modules which have been added interface correctly with the rest of the system.

1.6 THE ISO 9000 SERIES OF STANDARDS

The standard is important as it is becoming the main way in which customers can judge the competence of a software developer. It has been adopted for use by over 130 countries. One of the problems with the ISO 9001 series standard is that it is not industry-specific: it is expressed in general terms, and can be interpreted by the developers of diverse products such as ball-bearings, hair dryers, automobiles, sports equipment and televisions as well as software. A number of documents have been produced which relate the standard to the software industry, but do not go into a huge amount of detail. For the software industry the relevant standards are:

- *ISO 9001 Quality Systems—Model for Quality Assurance in Design, Development, Production, Installation and Servicing*. This is a standard which describes the quality system used to support the development of a product which involves design.
- *ISO 9000-3 Guidelines for the Application of ISO 9001 to the Development, Supply and Maintenance of Software*. This is a specific document which interprets ISO 9001 for the software developer.
- *ISO 9004-2 Quality Management and Quality System Elements—Part 2*. This document provides guidelines for the servicing of software and facilities such as user support.

Each country has a specific instantiation of the ISO 9000 series of standards, for example in the United Kingdom the standard is known as BS5750. The requirements of the standard are partitioned into 20 headings:

Inspection, measuring and test equipment	Management responsibility
Quality system	Inspection and test status
Control of nonconforming product	Contract review
Design control	Corrective action
Handling, storage, packaging and delivery	Document control
Purchasing	Quality records
Purchaser supplied product	Internal quality audits
Product identification and traceability	Training
Process control	Servicing
Inspection and testing	Statistical techniques

Each chapter of this book corresponds to one of these headings.

1.7 ATTAINING ISO 9001 ACCREDITATION

The process of becoming ISO 9001 accredited will differ from country to country. This section describes how it is achieved within the United Kingdom using the British Standards Institute (BSI) as the accreditation body. While this section is most relevant to British readers, it will still be useful to other readers as accreditation is carried out in a similar way in many other countries.

The first event that occurs is that a company decides it wants accreditation. It contacts the BSI who send a questionnaire to the company asking for basic details required to start the accreditation process off. The information included on the questionnaire will consist of items such as the number of employees in the company, the nature of the company, and those parts of the company for which registration is not being sought. For companies which are not very advanced in terms of quality assurance advice is normally given at this stage from the BSI about seminars, training and consultancy which is available from a number of sources. One form of advice is provided by the BSI pre-assessment visit scheme. Here an audit team from the BSI concentrates on those areas of a company's quality system where their time can be of maximum benefit to the company. It effectively carries out an informal audit of the existing quality system and produces a written report listing deficiencies.

When a company feels it is ready for assessment it makes an application to the BSI who appoint an employee to control the subsequent process of assessment. The next step is then for the BSI to examine the company's quality management system documentation at the BSI's premises. The results from this are included in a report which details those areas of the quality system that require modification in order to conform to ISO 9001.

The next stage is for the BSI to appoint an assessment team to visit the company. Normally this visit will occur after at least three months of operation of the quality system in order that, for example, sufficient evidence of the effective auditing of projects has occurred. At the end of the assessment visit the team will make one of three recommendations:

- Unqualified recommendation for registration.
- Qualified recommendation for registration. This usually means that some form of corrective action is required by the company and some limited reassessment by the BSI has to take place.
- No recommendation for registration. This usually means that the quality system is still seriously deficient and requires a full reassessment.

Once any corrective actions have taken place the quality system is passed, a certificate is issued, the company is entered on the British Department of Trade and Industry's Register of Companies holding ISO 9000 certification, and an entry is placed in the BSI buyers' guide.

Once a company has been certified, the BSI operate a policy of continuing assessment. Normally, BSI QA assessors will visit the company between two and four times per year to carry out a partial reassessment which checks that the company is adhering to their quality system and that project quality plans are being followed. For software the BSI is currently required to perform a full reassessment every three years.

1.8 THE REMAINDER OF THIS BOOK

The remainder of this book is split into chapters, each of which describes a single section of the ISO 9001 standard and its relevance to software development. A chapter will contain a discussion of that section, describe the typical errors or problems that occur when a quality system does not conform to that section and conclude with a series of checks.

These checks are statements that you may want to read before improving your quality system to an ISO 9001 standard, or which may lead to questions that you may want to ask after you have improved your system. It is worth warning you that the statements are not exhaustive, and do not cover every detailed facet of every part of ISO 9001. However, if you feel that you have addressed each point in your company, then it means that your quality system has a good chance of conforming to the section of the standard being discussed in that chapter.

A subsidiary use for this series of checks is as a filter. If, before reading the chapter, you read this section and feel that your company has addressed all the items in the section, then there is little need for you to read the chapter.

Each chapter will give extracts from standards or procedures which embody the directives in the ISO 9001 standard. I have also included some examples of tips and techniques which can be used within an ISO 9001 environment. These are surrounded by boxes. Each chapter features a section which contains cross-references to ISO 9003. One of the features of ISO 9001 is the fact that a particular feature of a company's quality system, for example planning standards, has relevance to a number of sections of the standard.

1.9 SUMMARY

The main points embodied in this chapter are:

- A quality factor is some aspect of a software product which is important to the customer or developer. Sometimes it is important to both.
- A quality system is intended to ensure that quality factors identified at the beginning of a project are present in a completed software system.
- A standard is a description of the way in which a project document is structured and how information in the document is presented.
- A procedure is a set of instructions which describe how a particular software task should be carried out.
- A quality control is some activity which ensures that a particular quality factor is present in a software system and its associated documentation. It gives rise to documents which provide assurance that a particular quality factor is present.
- A quality manual is a document which contains standards, procedures and guidelines that can be adopted by a project manager for a particular software project.
- A quality plan embodies the standards, procedures and quality controls which are to be used on a project.
- ISO 9001 is an international standard which provides broad guidance to software developers on how to implement, maintain and improve a quality system capable of ensuring high-quality software.

2

MANAGEMENT RESPONSIBILITY

2.1 WHAT THIS PART OF THE STANDARD MEANS

This part of the standard is concerned with the fact that a company should have a quality system, that management should support that system and that a very senior member of staff should be responsible for the system.

2.2 SENIOR MANAGERIAL RESPONSIBILITY

The standard implies that a senior manager, usually at board level, should take responsibility for the quality system. This means that this member of staff should represent the quality function within high-level discussions of the company. This member of staff, who may have other responsibilities, should have the following QA-specific responsibilities:

- He or she should introduce regular agenda items at board level which concern quality assurance.
- He or she should introduce sporadic but important agenda items at board level which concern quality assurance. For example, ISO 9001 insists on a regular review of the quality system. The result of this review, in summary form, should be presented by this member of staff.
- The member of staff who is formally responsible for the day-to-day management of the quality assurance function reports to this senior member of staff.
- He or she is formally responsible at board level for any deficiencies and problems with the quality system.

- He or she is ultimately responsible for ironing out problems between the development function in a company and the quality assurance function. For example, an argument as to whether a particular project is repeatedly ignoring the quality controls that have been specified for it would reach this level of the company if the member of staff responsible for the day-to-day management of the quality system cannot resolve the problem. Most of these issues will never reach this level of the company. However, this member of staff is the person who resolves them—normally in favour of the quality assurance function.
- He or she is responsible for fielding questions and queries about the quality system at board level.
- He or she is responsible at board level for defining the level of funding required for the maintenance of the quality function and also making cases for increased funding arising from reviews of the quality system.
- If a project fails badly, then this senior member of staff should be responsible for any activities such as post-mortems which attempt to find out the reason for failure. Since a quality system is meant to be a repository of good practice, then a project failure should be regarded as a failure of the quality system or the staff who police it.

2.3 BOARD RESPONSIBILITY

The board of a company also has a responsibility for the quality system. The board of a company should ensure that enough resources are devoted to quality assurance and that they receive reports from the quality assurance function at all their board meetings. These reports should have a prominent position on the agenda and not be scheduled for the back end of the board meeting. There will be a number of different types of reports that they will receive. The first type will be regular reports on the functioning of the quality system. Since the quality system will contain standards and procedures governing activities such as planning and testing these reports will detail, in summary form, the external manifestations of the effectiveness of the quality system. For example, such reports will summarize levels of defect detection, time slippage and budget slippage for projects which are current, and the number and seriousness of errors being notified to staff who are maintaining the software systems which have been released to the customer.

Tips and techniques 1

A huge incentive for managers to adhere to a quality system, and not just concentrate on target delivery date and cost, is to shut down a project's budget account only after a year of two of maintenance has taken place. For bespoke systems there will normally be a team fielding errors from the purchaser. Any resource consumed in rectifying errors, up to a certain point in time, should be subtracted from the original project budget. In manager appraisal this is the figure which should be used to judge performance. If the budget has been exceeded, then two things might have occurred: first, the project manager may have badly estimated the project; or second, the quality system was not used properly.

The second type of report will be presented at irregular intervals and concern the maintenance and improvement of the quality system. Like a software system a quality system has to change. A number of factors give rise to changes. They are:

Changes in software technology For example, a new programming language would give rise to a requirement for a standard for that language.

Changes in business policy For example, a company who, in the past, produced bespoke software may be thinking of developing package-based software. This usually means that the standards and procedures which govern the process of changing a system— the discipline known as *configuration management*—have to be strengthened in order to cope with the potentially massive increase in system versions.

Changes in system architectures The best example of this has been the influence of the microprocessor. Over the last fifteen years the microprocessor has meant that the proportion of software to hardware in a system has increased dramatically, thus necessitating the strengthening of existing quality systems.

Changes in company policy For example, a board member may have attended a seminar on quality, and have persuaded other members of the board that, like Japanese companies, his or her board should receive regular summary reports on defects detected and the reasons for these defects.

2.4 DAY-TO-DAY RESPONSIBILITY

A company should designate one member of staff who is responsible for the day-to-day management of the quality system. In large companies this person will be the head of the quality assurance department. In a small company it would be a senior manager who would usually have other responsibilities such as being responsible for the business of a number of current projects. The member of staff who is responsible for quality assurance on a day-to-day basis has a number of responsibilities. They are:

- To manage the day-to-day activities of quality staff who are the link with the development projects. Such staff normally act in an auditing capacity for most of their time; however, in more enlightened companies they also have a more direct role in that they help project managers establish which quality controls are to be adopted on their projects.
- To monitor and control resources delegated to the quality assurance function by the board of the company.
- To resolve any problems which occur during the day-to-day running of projects. For example, a member of the quality staff may discover during the auditing of a project that the quality controls which have been agreed have not been complied with. The role of the quality manager is to step in and remind the project manager responsible that company policy is that quality controls have to be adhered to. If the quality controls are being ignored on a regular basis, then the quality manager has to send the problem upwards to the next tier of the company for resolution by the board member responsible for quality assurance.

- To be responsible for the receipt of quality data and the production of summary reports which are presented to the board of the company. Typical reports which would be produced would be histograms showing the extent and seriousness of errors discovered by customers.
- To be responsible for the career development of those members of the company who are involved in the development and maintenance of the quality system.
- To be responsible for the day-to-day management of projects which have been set up to review and improve the quality system. ISO 9001 is very keen on continually monitoring the effectiveness and relevance of a quality system. It is important that the most senior person in the quality function manages any review and improvement projects.

2.5 VERIFICATION RESOURCES AND PERSONNEL

Section 4.1.2.2 of the standard states that:

> The supplier shall identify in-house verification requirements, provide adequate resources and assign trained personnel for verification requirements.

This means that for all the tasks in the quality plan the developer should have documented these tasks, ensured that the staff who are to carry out quality control tasks such as system testing have enough experience and that adequate resource and time has been given to these tasks in the quality plan. If trained staff are not available, the quality plan should detail the training that untrained staff should undergo prior to carrying out quality control tasks. This part of the standard also stresses the fact that the staff who carry out quality control tasks should be independent of the staff who have direct responsibility for the work being performed.

Tips and techniques 2

One effective way of ensuring independence in programming is to involve two members of staff. The first programs the module. The second then has to listen while the first programmer explains the logic of the module. Even if the second programmer says nothing, the very act of describing a module to another programmer always seems to result in the first programmer discovering errors. When all the errors are rectified the second programmer then has to go away and test the module. This ensures that he or she actually listens to the narrative produced by the programmer. When the tests have finally been successful the second programmer signs-off the module as being correct. A crafty project manager will often assign the first programmer to another programmer who he or she respects, is in awe of, or fears. In this way the first programmer almost always delivers correct program code first time.

There are a number of ways in which independence can be implemented. First, it could mean that a senior member of staff checks some work such as a completed module and 'signs-off' that work as being of a satisfactory standard. The second way is to employ technical reviews in which a number of staff examine a particular product such as a requirements specification. The chair of the review signs-off the product as being correct and conforming to any relevant standards such as a programming standard.

2.6 HIGH-LEVEL POLICY STATEMENTS

It is important that the board of a company produces a high-level statement about the quality system. This policy statement should be given prominence in all the relevant company publications, should be the first OHP that newly appointed staff see on induction courses, and should be posted in prominent positions around company premises. The policy statement should not be too long. Most staff lose interest in policy statements which go into a massive amount of detail. An example of a good quality statement is:

> The revenues and profit of this company depend on the quality of the products which we produce. In order to ensure that this quality is at the very highest level we have a quality management system. This quality system contains standards, procedures and guidelines which represent the best developmental practice and have been devised to eliminate errors and deliver software on time. At the beginning of each project a manager will negotiate with the quality assurance department the level and nature of the quality controls that will be used on a project. We expect all members of staff from the board downwards to respect and adhere to these controls.

2.7 DOCUMENTED QUALITY SYSTEM

This part of the standard implies that there should be documented quality system. This system should match the description given in Section 1.1. There should be a quality manual which contains standards, procedures and guidelines. The quality manual should not only address developmental activities, but also quality assurance activities such as auditing. The first page of the manual should reproduce the board's policy statement on quality. The introductory chapter of the quality manual should describe the process whereby a manager identifies quality factors relevant to a project, and incorporates checks that these factors are present via quality controls. The quality system should be regularly reviewed for its effectiveness at least once a year.

It is important to stress that it is not sufficient to have a quality manual which is applied to every project irrespective of its nature. While this policy is better than doing nothing, it does not recognize that projects can differ by a large amount, and that the degree of quality control that should reflect this difference can vary enormously from project to project. For example, a project which develops safety-critical software with heavy real-time constraints for a hardware platform which is new will need a much higher degree of quality control than a project which develops simple clerical software for a PC. Thus, a quality manual should not only provide descriptions of procedures, standards and controls but also describe how the manual itself should be used.

2.8 TRAINING AND INDUCTION

Every member of staff who is hired by a company should undergo an induction programme which introduces the company and its developmental and quality assurance
practices. A major component of this induction should be an introduction to the quality
system. The topics that should be dealt with include: the role of the quality manual;
how the quality system works; how standards and procedures are constructed and what
they aim to do; mechanisms whereby staff can comment and put forward suggestions to
improve the quality system; and a description of some war stories which illustrate the
impact of poor quality provision.

Tips and techniques 3

Do not be afraid of telling your staff about war stories. Companies
should not feel bad about talking about past disasters. Staff get to know
about them anyway. Use stories about past project disasters to motivate
staff about the quality system. The first lecture about quality assurance
in an induction course should describe a failed project. The first half
of the lecture should describe all the problems that were encountered.
The second half would point out the parts of the quality manual which
ensure that the problems never happen again. A company which is able
to look at past project failures, learn from them, and never repeat them,
takes quality assurance seriously. Indeed, it is a good test to see whether
your staff are reviewing and updating a quality system based on past
experience by asking hard questions about past project failures and
whether the quality manual contains elements which can now prevent
them. By addressing project disasters you might start to get over to
your staff the fact that a quality system is only a repository of best
practice, rather than something which has been developed to stifle their
creativity.

It is important that it is stressed in the induction programme that quality assurance has
two aims: to increase the profit of a company and hence benefit individual members of
the department in terms of better career enhancement opportunities, bonuses and more
generous salaries; and to enhance the quality of life of development staff on a project.
For example, the induction programme should include a session on how standards and
procedures are developed. This can be potentially very boring. However, if it is driven by
showing how a standard is devised by examining all the errors and irritations that occur
on a software project, then new staff will see that the quality system can be of great help
to them.

   An important point to put forward in any training programme is that the quality
manual represents best practice and has been distilled from a number of years' experience
of both good and bad projects. It is in effect a description of how a company carries out
development and quality assurance, and should be given to every inductee on their first
day.

2.9 RELATION TO ISO 9000-3

Section 4.1 of ISO 9000-3 is mainly a restatement of this part of ISO 9000-1. However, it does include some direction to the purchaser of a software product about working within the standard. Its main implications are that:

- A purchaser's representative be appointed as soon as possible to deal with the process of liaising with the developer over purchaser requirements. This person should not only be responsible for the definition of requirements, but should also be the first point of call for any queries from the supplier. Ideally, there should be no substitution of the purchaser's representative during a project.
- The purchaser's representative should be responsible for answering questions from the supplier. These not only include questions about requirements but also more mundane matters such as the physical arrangements for staff who are to visit the purchaser's location, the availability of purchaser's equipment and planning details such as the location and timing of liaison meetings.
- The purchaser's representative should have the power to approve any of the supplier's proposals. For example, if the supplier wishes to change a project plan slightly to delay the delivery of an item and move forward the delivery of another item, then the purchaser's representative should have the power to agree to this.
- The purchaser's representative ensures that any assumptions and agreements made between the supplier and the purchaser are kept. For example, the project plan may have stated that the purchaser will review and sign-off any documentation within a specified period. The purchaser's representative should ensure that this is held to.
- The purchaser's representative should be responsible for defining the acceptance test criteria. These are statements which will, eventually, give rise to acceptance tests that will govern whether the purchaser will take delivery of the developed system.
- The purchaser's representative should be the person who liaises with the supplier when delivered software or software components are produced by the supplier which do not meet requirements.

The role of any purchaser's representative should be defined in the project plan, together with the expectations that the supplier has of the representative. There is no implication in the standard that one person will carry out all the purchaser's representative's tasks; there is, perhaps, the implication that one person should be the contact point within the purchaser's company.

Another part of Section 4.1 of the ISO 9000-3 guide describes the fact that joint reviews should be held between the purchaser and the supplier. Some of these reviews would be progress meetings; however, some of them will deal with technical issues which are specific to customer requirements. This means that there should be a review which considers the statement of requirements produced by the purchaser together with a review of the requirements specification which emerges from the process of analysing the statement of requirements. Other reviews would normally cover topics such as the acceptance tests which are to be applied to the software that is to be developed.

2.10 PROBLEMS

If this section of ISO 9001 is not adhered to, then major problems occur which affect all parts of the company. A list of the problems is:

* A quality system which is used at the whim of individual project managers leads to poor software product being delivered. Good managers will employ the quality system well. Poor managers will only use those aspects of the quality system which they believe will not hinder the delivery of a system on time and to budget. Normally the latter type of manager will deliver on time and to budget; however, the software that their projects produce will usually be error-ridden.
* A company without a quality manual does not have a central reference document which describes to new staff how software is developed in that company. Valuable time will need to be spent in communicating this information.
* Without standards and procedures, development tasks will be carried out in an ad hoc way. Good staff will, as a matter of course, use best practices. Poor staff will not. Since one error can kill a software system this will result in errors and late delivery— even if a project employs good staff.
* Without directions about addressing quality factors and using quality controls relevant to these factors, project managers are in danger of either having too many quality controls on a project or, more likely, too few.
* Without support for a quality system at a high level in a company few members of staff will take the quality system seriously.
* A company which does not regularly review its quality system will discover that it will become irrelevant to their technical and business needs very quickly.
* A company which does not have a specified director responsible for quality will have major difficulties in communicating business policy changes which affect the quality system to quality assurance staff.
* If regular reports are not being received at the board level from the quality assurance function, then the board is unable to sanction major resources to improve the quality system.
* If the company does not have a designated member of staff responsible for the day-to-day running of the quality system, then there will be little, if any, control over projects; there will be inadequate information flow to the board; the development of medium-term quality assurance policy will be ignored; and little career development for quality assurance staff will take place.
* If the company does not have a designated member of staff responsible for the day-to-day running of the quality system, then staff will feel that the communication gap between them and the board is so large that there is little point in carrying out activities such as providing suggestions to improve the quality system.
* If the company does not have a designated member of staff responsible for the day-to-day running of the quality system, then developmental staff will feel that quality assurance is not taken too seriously by the company.
* Without a central member of staff worrying about quality system improvement , there is a reduced probability that the quality system will evolve in harmony with changes in software technology and changes in company policy.

- Without backing from the board, via a high-level policy statement which is prominently displayed, development staff will feel that the company does not take quality assurance seriously.
- Without an adequate induction programme which seriously addresses the training of staff on quality assurance topics a company will experience a cynicism about the role of quality assurance from their staff. A cynicism embodied in the remark I heard once from a programmer that 'the role of quality assurance in this company is to stifle our creativity'.

2.11 CHECKS

The following should be found in a system which is certified to ISO 9001:

- A documented quality system containing standards and procedures, together with descriptions of quality controls and their associated documentation, and instructions on how to apply these quality controls.
- A designated member of the board of a company is responsible for quality assurance.
- Quality reports are a major agenda item at meetings of the board of directors.
- Adequate levels of resource are delegated to the quality assurance function.
- Regular reviews of the quality system which are aimed at checking its effectiveness.
- A designated member of staff is responsible for the day-to-day running of the quality system.
- Regular audits of projects to check whether agreed quality controls are being followed.
- A high-level policy statement on software quality assurance is issued by the board of a company, with the statement being displayed prominently on company publications and premises.
- Every new member of staff undergoes an induction programme which contains a substantial amount of detail on the company's quality system.

QUALITY SYSTEM

3.1 INTRODUCTION

This part of the standard states that a developer must maintain a quality system. There is also the implication that individual projects, via their quality plans, must use facilities provided by the quality system. There is a further implication that the system should be maintained: that is, it should be continually reviewed. This is embodied in the first two parts of Section 4.2:

> The supplier shall establish and maintain a documented quality system as a means of ensuring that product conforms to specified requirements. This shall include:
>
> a) the preparation of documented quality system procedures and instructions in accordance with the requirements of this International Standard;
>
> b) the effective implementation of the documented quality system procedures and instructions.

3.2 QUALITY SYSTEM DOCUMENTATION

The first requirement is that the quality system should be documented. This means that a quality manual should lie at the core of the quality system. This manual should contain standards, procedures and guidelines governing all the activities which impinge on the software development process. This not only includes activities such as project planning, requirements analysis, system design and programming, but also quality assurance-related activities such as project auditing and the reporting of non-compliance with the quality system.

A major feature of the quality manual is that it should provide a spectrum of quality controls which can be applied to a project in order to ensure that a certain collection of quality factors relevant to the project is present in a developed system. Some typical quality controls, together with their associated documentary evidence, are:

- The application of a software tool to program code which checks that the code adheres to the company programming standard. The printout from the tool indicating that no violations have occurred would be the documentary evidence.
- The execution of a technical review which examines the design of a subsystem to check that it correctly reflects its specification. The minutes of this meeting, signed-off by the chair, would be the documentary evidence.
- The execution of a system test which checks out one of the functions of a system; the documentation associated with this important type of quality control would be the test reports which documented the fact that the test took place and the correct results were obtained.
- The results from a usability trial in which user errors were monitored and stored in a database. Such a trial is a useful means of providing confirmation that the usability quality factor is present to a certain degree. The documentation associated with this control might be the printout from a software tool summarizing the extent and type of error committed by users and demonstrating that an allowable margin occurred.
- A description of the data that is passed between a system and a proprietary spreadsheet which a customer wants connected to the system. The design of the interface, signed-off by a senior designer, would be the quality control which ensured that the interoperability quality factor was present.

A quality system would be seriously deficient if there was not a description of the quality controls available to the project manager. These controls are usually associated with standards, procedures and system documentation. For example, the first example described above would form part of a procedure which, indirectly, provides assurance that the correctness quality factor is present. Standards and procedures should not only be applicable to development tasks but should also be applicable to quality assurance activities. This includes activities such as:

Auditing Standards and procedures should describe how auditing is carried out: the frequency, the notice given, the selection of quality controls which are to be selected for auditing, and who should be present at an audit. They should also describe the format of reports used to report on an audit, for example how the number and extent of non-compliances might be expressed in diagrammatic form.

Non-compliance This should describe what happens when serious non-compliance of quality controls is detected during an audit. Normally, this will result in a report being sent to the member of staff who manages the day-to-day activities of the quality function. He or she then makes a decision on what action to take.

Establishing quality controls The next section describes how a project manager interacts with the quality system in establishing quality controls for a particular project. In more enlightened companies the establishment of these quality controls is carried out and agreed by the project manager and staff from the quality function. The quality manual should describe the role of quality staff in this process.

3.3 THE USE OF THE QUALITY SYSTEM

An important part of the quality manual should be a section which describes how a quality plan is developed. This will describe the process whereby a project manager looks at a future project and decides how many quality controls are to be built in to a project and when they are to be applied. These will be incorporated in the quality plan for the project.

The quality manual should guide the project manager by offering guidelines, lists of quality factors, a step-by-step description of what to do to in order to identify quality factors, and also the relevant quality controls to be applied which are specific to a particular quality factor.

The quality manual will often provide advice about quality controls which is partly based on the result of a risk analysis. This risk analysis, which is normally driven by a series of questionnaires, examines factors such as: the level of knowledge of computing of the customer; the application area; the experience of the staff who are to be assigned to the project; the novelty of the hardware and software which is to be used; the project organization; and whether there are any stringent requirements for aspects of the system, such as its real-time response.

A project which has a relatively inexperienced team, uses new hardware and software, liaises with other development projects in distant countries, has to liaise with a customer who does not understand the nature of software technology, and has stringent memory and response-time requirements, will have quite a different set of quality controls from a small project developing software on a well-established computer such as a PC for a well-understood application area such as stock-control. Before leaving this section it is worth examining the nature of the quality controls on a project through a number of examples.

The first example concerns the project which is contracted to use an item of hardware which is still under development. The developer of the hardware has produced a software simulation of the hardware for use during the first three months of the project, after which the first delivery of the hardware will occur. Now, based on a risk analysis, the project manager will implement a number of actions which minimize the effect of late delivery or even delivery of hardware which does not conform to the simulator, for example by directing the legal department to place a large penalty clause in the contract with the supplier for late or poor delivery. As well as this, the project manager will install a quality control which checks that the hardware conforms to the simulator that was provided. Normally this quality control is embodied in a series of pre-delivery acceptance tests where the simulator and the hardware are run in parallel. The documentation which demonstrates that this quality control has been applied correctly is the test report from staff charged with checking the hardware.

The next example concerns a software system which is to be delivered to a customer who has little, if any, experience of dealing with a software developer. After carrying out a risk analysis, and speaking to the customer, the project manager may decide that there is a heavy risk of the customer continually changing his or her mind during the analysis process. In this case, the project manager may instigate a very heavy configuration management system for his or her project which has detailed costing procedures built into it for estimating the monetary effect of a change. For most projects, with experienced customers, these costing procedures would be omitted. However, the manager might feel that the extra effort involved in costing proposed changes would keep the project working to profit and also discourage the customer from making frivolous changes. The documentation for this quality control would be the detailed records which show the communication with the customer, the appraisal of the change by the developer and the costing calculations produced by the staff in charge of configuration management.

The third example concerns the implementation of a quality control on a project which plans to deliver a commercial data processing system that has a very stringent response-time requirement. The project manager may decide that the requirement is so stringent that the project is structured into two parts: a pre-development part which produces an early version that can be used as a performance prototype, and a development part which delivers the final, production version of the system. The performance prototype would be used to explore response-time issues; for example, it may be used to negotiate which functions should be implemented and which functions omitted from a customer wish-list in order to achieve performance. For this form of development a number of quality controls would be used. For example: a standard which described how the discussion between the customer and developer over functionality versus response time proceeded and was agreed; or a quality control which provides evidence that performance testing was carried out adequately, not only with respect to accurate measurements being taken, but also with respect to the correct version of the performance prototype being used.

This part of the quality manual should also describe the format of the quality plan: the description of the quality controls, who carries out the quality controls and when they are to be applied.

Tips and techniques 4

One of the major things I look for in a good quality management system is *traceability*. This is the ability to move effortlessly from a document or program code to other related documents and program code. As you will see later this is vitally important for system design and requirements specification. However, it is also important for planning. The quality plan will detail the quality tasks which are part of a project and the project plan will detail developmental tasks. You should instigate some sort of numbering convention which allows you to look at a particular developmental task such as the programming of a module and cross-reference it to a quality task.

3.4 THE IMPROVEMENT OF THE QUALITY SYSTEM

Although the improvement of the quality system is dealt with later in the standard in a little more detail, this section of the standard does refer to this process. For example, Section 4.2 states that timely consideration needs to be given to:

> The updating, as necessary, of quality control, inspection and testing techniques, including the development of new instrumentation.

While the reference to instrumentation is obviously only relevant to conventional engineering, there is still the implication here of quality system improvement.

A number of companies have expended a large amount of resource in installing expensive quality systems which have remained in place for many years without any modification to them taking place. This is a mistake—a mistake which becomes increasingly costly as time proceeds. There are a number of reasons—over and above the very pragmatic one that the ISO 9001 series insists on it—why a company should be monitoring, reviewing and evolving their quality system: examining patterns of non-adherence to the system; examining where software errors have occurred; looking at the effect that new technology has on the quality system; and discovering whether changes in business strategy will have an effect. There are a number of reasons why the operation of a quality system should be continually monitored and improved:

- There will always be a tendency for staff to skimp in terms of their adherence to the quality system. This is not because they are unprofessional; it is more because there is a pressure on staff to deliver on time and to budget. Staff in a hurry to deliver a system may ignore parts of a quality plan. If a company is certified to ISO 9001, then a record of serious non-adherence is enough for the certification to be invalidated.
- The first version of a quality standard is never perfect. There will be parts of the system which still allow an unacceptable level of errors or require staff to carry out too much work. It is important during the early stages of the use of a quality system that particular care is taken in monitoring what are perceived to be these weak spots. Even quality systems which have been in place for a number of years contain processes which can be considerably improved.
- New software technology can give rise to extra requirements for the quality system. For example, a new notation for expressing the design of a real-time system will necessitate the development of standards which govern the layout of the notation and procedures for validating documents expressed in the notation. It is important that these new requirements are detected in advance of the implementation of any new technology.
- Changes in business policy and strategy can give rise to the need for major changes in a quality system. For example, a company whose main business is producing bespoke software may decide that, with users increasingly looking to package-based solutions, the time has come to develop software packages which can be tailored by the company for a specific customer's requirements. This could have two major impacts on the developer. First, there will be need to tighten up the configuration management parts of the quality manual; these parts may be adequate for bespoke system development but, almost invariably, are inadequate for a situation where there are a large number of versions of a system in existence. Second, design standards and procedures will need to be tightened in order to cope with techniques such as table-driven development that are used for producing packages.

3.5 THE QUALITY IMPROVEMENT TEAM

One strategy which can be adopted to cope with the improvement and evolution of the quality system is to appoint a quality improvement team. Their brief is to continually examine the functioning of the quality system, business policy and technological developments and to specify tasks that need to be carried out in order to evolve the quality system.

Such a team would come from diverse areas in a company. It is important that it contain a senior member of the company—preferably at board level. The reason for this is that it is important that senior management show their commitment to improvement of the quality system; after all, they are users of the quality system. One of the group should, preferably, have had experience of maintaining a system: it is with this activity that the need for quality assurance is at its greatest.

Tips and techniques 5

When you are improving a quality system pay particular attention to what the staff involved in maintenance say. These staff see the worst part of the quality system manifested in poor requirements specifications, incomplete designs and poorly structured program code. Also, if you have staff who you feel are not in sympathy with the quality system and, say, continually ignore standards and procedures, then give them some maintenance to do. You will find that, more often than not, these staff will come back as QA zealots.

A project manager should also be part of the group. Project management use different parts of a quality system from those which senior management and technical staff use. A member of technical staff, say a designer or analyst, should also be part of the group together with a programmer who currently works on the maintenance of a system. If the company is large, then it may have an R & D department. If so, then a member of that department should be part of the group: an important input into the deliberations of the group is an indication of technologies which will affect the company and which are just over the horizon. If the R & D department are doing their job, then they should be continually monitoring and disseminating the spread and effect of new technology. The final member of the group should come from the quality assurance department.

The group will base their deliberations on a number of inputs. An exhaustive list is shown here, though it is important to point out that it would be wildly optimistic to assume that every one of them will be used, even for the most sophisticated software developer:

- Project debriefing reports. A quality system should have a standard and procedure which directs a project manager to fill in a questionnaire after a project has been completed. Such questionnaires are a useful repository of experiences and an important component of such documents are questions about the effectiveness of the quality system.
- Reports on technology which will affect the company in one, two and five year time spans. As mentioned previously, these reports should emerge from the R & D department. If the company is too small to support such a department then the reports should be commissioned from external consultants.

- Reports from validation activities. For example, reviews which detail the extent and level of errors that are being discovered at each phase of a project. These reports will not be read in a raw form, but will be presented to the group in summary form. Normally staff who are charged with the quality function will carry out limited post-mortems on these reports and provide some indication of the reasons why certain categories of error have occurred.
- Summaries of audit reports from quality staff which indicate where deviations from the quality system are occurring.
- Unsolicited letters from staff on projects who, for example, may be having trouble using a standard.
- Business policy statements from the board of directors.
- Questionnaires filled in by staff asking them about their perceptions of the effectiveness of the quality system.
- If the company has implemented quality circles, then reports from these quality circles should be used.
- The contents of suggestion boxes.
- Reports from consultants who have been called in to periodically review the quality system.
- Reports from staff who provide a servicing function. Such staff will have a good idea of some of the problems with a software system, for example the poorness of an interface, which may be ascribed to deficiencies in the quality system.
- Reports from quality staff who have traced back selections of errors which have been detected during validation to their source. It is important to point out that this is quite a time-consuming activity and only a small selection of errors can be treated in this way. Nevertheless if it is possible to produce this report then it can be very valuable indeed.

Tips and techniques 6

One technique which has been used to test out the effectiveness of one part of a quality system is known as *bebugging*. It is applied to technical reviews using program code. The quality assurance department intercepts any program code which is to be reviewed and inserts a number of artificial errors in the code. They then examine the documentation of the completed code review and discover how many of the artificial errors have been discovered. The percentage of these errors discovered can be regarded as a measure of either the effectiveness of those parts of the quality system oriented to code reviews or the efficiency of the staff involved. Obviously further research would be needed in order to discover any reasons for a lack of efficiency.

3.6 RELATION TO ISO 9000-3

Section 4.2 stresses the fact that a company should always have a documented quality system and that elements of the quality system, extracted from the quality manual, should be placed in a quality plan and redeveloped on a project-by-project basis. The quality plan should be a dynamic document and should be reviewed and agreed by all the participants in the project: customer, supplier and any subcontractors. The implication here is that the quality plan should be a contractual document and the quality plans produced by subcontractors should mesh in with that produced by the supplier.

An important point made by ISO 9000-3 in Section 4.2.1 is that quality should pervade the whole of a project and should not be the sole province of staff involved in system and acceptance testing. The implication here is that quality activities such as requirements reviews, prototyping, simulation, and performance studies, which normally take place in the early stages of a project, should be used where necessary.

Sections 5.5.1 and 5.5.2 provide guidance on the form of the quality plan, that it should: list the quality factors (objectives) and describe exit and entry criteria for each activity; detail all the testing, verification and validation activities for a project; and outline the specific responsibilities of the suppliers' staff, the developers' staff and sub-contract staff for quality activities and configuration management. It should also detail activities associated with the analysis of defects and any remedial activities which are necessary to correct software which does not conform to its specification.

3.7 PROBLEMS

The problems which are encountered if this part of the standard is not adhered to are very serious:

- Without a documented quality system the application of quality controls, standards and procedures are an ad hoc process resulting in huge variabilities in the quality of software delivered from project to project.
- An undocumented quality system means that conscientious project managers can spend valuable time making up standards and procedures for their own projects. There will be the risk that these will not be of the highest standard, since the specific expertise of quality assurance staff might not be used.
- Without directions on how to use the quality system in order to develop a quality plan, there is the danger that existing standards and procedures will be used without taking into account project-specific factors. This means that quality factors such as reliability and interoperability will not be adequately taken into account.
- A quality system which is not continually reviewed will eventually become out of date because of changes in software technology, hardware technology, and modifications to a company's business and corporate policy.
- An undocumented quality system sends clear messages to staff about the attitude of a company to quality assurance.
- If a quality system is undocumented then there is no documentation to give to staff, say during induction, which describes how a company manages projects, develops software and applies quality assurance. This would result in the training department developing documentation which would not be needed if the quality system was properly documented. A good check on the quality of a quality manual is whether you feel that it can be given to new, raw staff who join your company.

- If projects are not adequately audited according to the quality controls agreed by the project manager and the quality assurance function, then there is a temptation to omit the controls by the manager in a quest for early or on-time delivery of the software product at the expense of quality.

3.8 CHECKS

- A quality manual exists which is given to every member of staff and which acts as a description of how the company manages projects, develops software and applies quality controls.
- A quality manual which contains standards and procedures for *every* developmental, managerial and quality assurance activity—even those, such as prototyping, which may be performed infrequently.
- Regular reviews of the quality system which take, as their input, a number of sources including project debriefings, reports from maintenance staff and R & D reports.
- Regular audits of projects are carried out by quality staff to check for adherence to the agreed quality controls that are embodied in the quality plan.
- A standard and procedure for the quality plan which details its format and how it is to be produced. This usually involves the project manager carrying out a risk analysis and is a by-product of the process of organizing and planning a project.
- A member of the board is responsible for quality system improvement.
- There is a formal group responsible for improvement of the quality system.
- Guidance exists for selecting adequate quality controls for a project.
- A substantial amount of time on training courses for new staff is spent on the quality system.
- Every project uses its own quality plan—it does not just take the quality manual off the shelf.

4

CONTRACT REVIEW

4.1 INTRODUCTION

The contract for a software system will contain a large amount of legal and technical information. This part of the ISO 9001 standard is concerned with directives to a system supplier to ensure that the contract can be met, and that any changes to the contract agreed by the supplier and the purchaser are documented. Section 4.3 of the standard states that:

> Each contract shall be reviewed by the supplier to ensure that
>
> a) the requirements are adequately defined and documented;
> b) any requirements differing from those in the tender are resolved;
> c) the supplier has the capability to meet contractual requirements.

There is also a requirement that the software supplier ensures that the contract can be met: that a specified product can be delivered with all its requirements satisfied within the time-scales specified by the purchaser and to a specified cost. There are a number of models of contracting in the software industry, and this part of the standard should govern the software supplier's behaviour when he or she participates in any of them. Three common models are:

- The purchaser produces a wish list of requirements for a system—known as a *statement of requirements*—and then asks a number of companies to tender for the system. Each of these companies produces a document which, as well as containing glossy brochures describing their software prowess, also contains a description of an outline solution and a tendered cost. Increasingly, purchasers are also demanding a sight of the company's documented quality system and this is often enclosed with bidding documents. The purchaser then selects one of these companies based on a number of factors, including technical competence and cost.

- Tendering occurs, as in the first case, but the number of companies who have bid for the software contract are whittled down to a few—normally three. Each company is then paid to produce more detailed documentation such as a project plan and an outline requirements specification. The purchaser then selects the supplier, again based on expertise and cost.
- A contract is tendered for by a number of software suppliers. The purchaser awards a two-stage contract where the first contract is a feasibility study for which the supplier examines the purchaser's wish list, and considers whether they are implementable under the constraints specified by the purchaser. These constraints will include overall cost, the hardware base and the required delivery date. The report produced by the supplier will either say the system can be built, cannot be built, or can be built if some constraints are relaxed, for example by dropping some of the functionality. Based on the result of this study the purchaser may decide not to proceed with the system, place the contract with the supplier, or restart the tendering process whereby the documents produced by the company who carried out the feasibility study are used to provide information to the new tendering companies.

It is important to point out that there are a number of variants of these models, but that whatever variant is used, this section of ISO 9001 determines the supplier's behaviour. There is also the case where no contract is involved, or at least only some form of informal agreement is in existence. This normally occurs when the computer department of a company produces a software system for another part of the company. While the business trend is towards internal contracts and the concept of the internal purchaser, there are still a number of computer service departments producing software without any formal notion of a contract. Even so, the software department which has a quality system certified to ISO 9001 should behave as professionally as an external software company which is similarly certificated, even to the point of instigating an internal version of the contracting process.

4.2 STANDARDS AND PROCEDURES FOR FEASIBILITY ANALYSIS

A major concern of this section of the standard is that the software supplier should, before formally starting a project, be confident that software contracted for can be delivered within the constraints specified by the purchaser. These constraints will be various and include system-specific constraints such as response time, memory occupancy limits, file occupancy limits, compatibility with other software or hardware, and the satisfaction of a set of functional requirements. They will also contain specific project constraints such as required duration and required cost. There will also be a large number of other, indirect factors which have to be considered. For example, the purchaser may state that since his or her staff are very busy they can only spare one member of staff for project liaison for one hour per month. The software supplier must then decide whether this would lead to other constraints such as delivery time not being satisfied.

This means that the supplier needs standards and procedures for determining project feasibility. These standards and procedures will cover the following activities:

Outline project planning At such an early stage in a project there is a need for the software supplier to calculate a rough cost for the project. A major input into this process is the amount of staff time that is required. Consequently, the supplier should have standards and procedures which enable the tasks in the project to be identified and approximate costs given. These tasks will be at a high level, for example *Design subsystem A*, and would be considerably expanded into subtasks if the project proceeds. In order for this planning to take place the supplier should have carried out some form of outline requirements analysis and design.

Outline requirements analysis and design A major input into the process of carrying out an initial costing is to determine the amount of manpower needed for a particular project. The level of effort will depend on the tasks which are carried out which, again, depends on the architecture of the system. At this stage of a project there is no real need for a software supplier to carry out a full design. However, in order to identify the nature and extent of high-level tasks an outline requirements analysis and system design needs to be carried out. The software supplier should have standards and procedures which describe how this process is carried out and how the results are documented.

Technical analysis It is important that the supplier's quality manual contains standards and procedures which govern the process of determining whether a system is technically feasible. For example, a purchaser may require a system with harsh response-time constraints. A good way of determining whether these constraints can be satisfied is by developing a performance prototype. The quality manual should provide guidelines which govern the development of such a prototype. Other technical factors which the quality manual should address include the calculation of file size, memory occupancy and reliability.

Outline cost determination Cost is a major constraint on projects. At the pre-contractual stage there should be adequate standards and procedures in existence which provide help to the software supplier in calculating a contractual cost. These standards and procedures should also describe the level to which costing should be calculated. For example, the project may be very similar to a previous project. In this case a very perfunctory costing could be carried out. However, the project may be regarded as so novel that a full costing may need to be carried out. The guidelines for costing should provide guidance on the level of costing adopted. There should be a procedure which helps staff to establish whether an outline cost is correct. For example, the quality manual should contain instructions to staff to check the estimated cost with similar systems which have been developed in the past.

4.3 STANDARDS AND PROCEDURES FOR RISK ANALYSIS

Every project involves a degree of risk. When a software supplier carries out the process of determining whether a project can be carried out within a number of constraints, it is important that some determination of the risks inherent in the project is carried out. These risks will be multifarious, and involve personnel-based risks such as a key member of staff leaving, technical risks such as having to use a hardware base which the supplier is unfamiliar with and external risks such as subcontractor not delivering on time. It is important that the quality manual contains risk-analysis procedures.

These procedures are normally driven by a questionnaire which contains a list of the most likely risks which the company thinks will occur. A fragment from such a questionnaire is:

3.4 Customer-specific risk factors

- Is this the first time that we have dealt with this customer?
- Is this the first time the customer has involved itself with an external contractor?
- Is this the first time that such an application has been computerized for the customer?
- Have the customer's staff who will liaise with the project been nominated?
- Are the customer's staff who will liaise with the project knowledgeable about the application area?
- Are the customer's staff who will liaise with the project knowledgeable about the computer technology?

The quality manual should offer directives about how this questionnaire is used and how the overall risk of the project is gauged, and provide advice on how to mitigate risk. For example, if the project manager thinks that there is a very high probability that a designer will leave in mid-project, then the project will be organized in such a way that the designer would work with a talented, junior member of staff who can take over if the risk becomes concrete. The results of the risk analysis will be used by the supplier's management to decide whether the project is initiated or bid for, and is often used to determine a level of extra resourcing which ensures a profit even if the most likely risks occur.

Tips and techniques 7

It is a good idea to have a company disaster list. This list would contain all the bad events that have happened to software projects over the years, including events which can be laid at a purchaser's door and events which were out of the control of the supplier. This list can be initially created by asking project managers to remember the bad things about their past projects. It can be updated by asking staff in project debriefings if any problems occurred during the project. This list of bad events can be read by a project manager in order to jog his or her mind about some of the risks that could happen in a project and has the effect of concentrating the mind during the process of risk analysis.

4.4 THE REQUIREMENTS AUDIT TRAIL

Before a project is initiated there will be a period during which the supplier and the purchaser will discuss requirements and a requirements specification will be produced. The level of detail in this document will depend on the nature of the contracting process. If the supplier is bidding against a number of other contractors, then an outline requirements specification will be produced. If the software supplier is sure of the contract, but worried over the overall cost of the project, a more detailed requirements specification will be produced which can be used for accurate costing. Whatever level of requirements specification is produced, it is important that the quality manual provides facilities for establishing and maintaining an audit trail, from the initial statement of requirements to the full requirements specification. An example of a procedure which enables the audit trail to be maintained is shown here. It is taken from a procedure which concerns the development of a requirements specification:

4.5 Modifications to the requirements specification

During a project the requirements specification will change. After it has been frozen any changes will be subject to the configuration management practices that the project has adopted (see Section 6.2). However, there will be a period before freezing when change will be very dynamic, but will need to be documented. A customer will normally provide us with a statement of requirements and we will derive the requirements specification. During this period a large number of change requests will come from the customer with some emerging from our side. It is important that these modifications are written down in case of dispute later in the project. It is worth stressing that the project should only accept change proposals from customer's staff who have been authorized to make these changes. The identity of such staff can be found in the project plan.

Meetings with the customer will always be minuted and the minutes sent to the customer for agreement. Normally project managers will have inserted some time limit in the project plan, after which, if there is no customer response, we will assume that the minutes have been agreed to.

There will also be less formal means of communication used. Even if the customer used such means as a telephone call to request changes, it is vitally important that a record is kept of the change and a letter sent to the customer representative on the project confirming the change.

That is, it must be theoretically possible to track from the initial statement of requirements to the requirements specification which is issued as the base document for the development part of the project. It is also worth stressing that it is vitally important to track changes to the requirements specification during the development project.

Tips and techniques 8

Always express your documentation in an hierarchic way. This is most important when developing the requirements specification. For the functional part of this specification, partition the functional description into functions, subfunctions, sub-subfunctions and so on. If you do this, then staff—both from the purchaser and the supplier—are able to concentrate on one section of the functional specification at a time without getting other parts of the functional specification intruding. For example, a purchasing manager who is liaising with the supplier's staff and checking out the part of the requirements specification concerned with his or her function does not want details intruding from other functions such as accounting and delivery.

To implement this tracking the quality manual should insist on some cross-referencing from the statement of requirements to the functions and constraints contained in the requirements specification. For many statements of requirements this audit trail is very difficult to establish initially since many purchasers produce vague initial documents. What is normally done in this case is for the supplier to produce an outline version of this statement of requirements which imposes some structure on the statement of requirements. The process of eliciting enough purchaser requirements necessary for activities such as costing can then back-reference this document.

Usually at this stage in a project the audit trail will be simple: both functions and constraints are given unique names in either the statement of requirements if it is good enough, or the supplier's version of the statement if it is not. Any changes will then unambiguously reference the functions and constraints which are changed.

4.5 PROJECT BIDDING

The quality manual should have a major section which describes the process of bidding for a project, whatever model of contracting is used. This is the part of the quality manual which brings together all the activities detailed in this section, activities such as risk analysis, purchaser contact, the establishment of a requirements change audit trail and the development of bidding documentation.

The quality manual should detail what should be included as base information in any bidding documentation. Obviously every purchaser will have specific requirements for what is included in a bid; however, much of the information in a bidding document will be common from purchaser to purchaser. For example, it is good practice to place a list of successful contracts in the bidding documentation, either as a glossy insert or as information which is word-processed into the bid.

The quality manual should also contain standards and procedures for a formal review of a bidding document. This will include who should attend such a review, how problems are documented and also a checklist which guides the reviewers through the process of reading the bid prior to attending the review.

4.6 FORMAL CONTRACT REVIEW

When a supplier is successful in being awarded a contract for a software project a formal contract is normally issued and signed by all parties. It is vitally important that all aspects of the contract are reviewed—both legal and technical. If the supplier has had to develop a formal bid document, then a review should have been held which checks this document for correctness. In theory, then, much of the material in contractual documents, such as an improved statement of requirements or requirements specification, will have been the subject of rigorous scrutiny. However, in the period between the submission of the bid document and the drafting of the contract quite a large amount of change could have occurred. For example, a purchaser may have had some hopelessly ambitious expectations about the extent of the software that could be developed for the price that they expected to pay. In this case the company may have selected a supplier that could deliver the system which has the closest functionality, with the expectation that a large amount of negotiation would occur regarding the statement of requirements prior to the signing of a contract.

Because of the possibility of change there should be a formal review of the contract. The quality manual will contain standards, procedures and checklists which determine the conduct of this meeting and the format of the documentation produced. This review should involve legal, managerial and technical aspects.

> **Tips and techniques 9**
>
> Always give reasons for directives in the quality manual. For example,
> in describing why an audit trail of requirements changes should be kept,
> mention the fact that the company almost went to costly litigation over
> some changes which a customer insisted on, which were never docu-
> mented and which, in the end, the customer denied all knowledge of.
> Computer staff are usually happy to follow standards and procedures,
> *provided they are told the reason why.*

4.7 RELATION TO ISO 9000-3

ISO 9000-3 is full of good advice about what this part of the standard means. Section 5.2.1 describes the information that needs to be examined during contract review. This includes the contract scope, any risks in the development process, the supplier's responsibility *vis-à-vis* subcontractors and any specialized terminology to be used by both parties.

Section 5.2.2 details the items which are normally regarded as contractual. These include: the acceptance criteria used to determine whether the purchaser will take delivery of a system; the way in which purchaser's requirements changes which occur during development will be processed; the purchaser's role in requirements specification and acceptance; any facilities provided by the purchaser; and the quality plan that will be employed.

Section 5.3 stresses the fact that the requirements specification should be developed in close cooperation between the purchaser and the supplier. The requirements specification should:

> ... have a complete, unambiguous set of functional requirements. In addition, these requirements
> should include all aspects necessary to satisfy the purchaser's need. These may include, but are not
> limited to, the following: performance, safety, reliability, security and privacy. These requirements
> should be stated precisely enough so as to allow validation during acceptance.

The important thing to stress is the fact that there should be enough precision in the requirements specification that staff who are to check out the system via activities such as acceptance testing can derive adequate checks and tests.

Section 5.3.2 stresses the communication aspects of the process of developing a requirements specification. It states that issues which must be addressed in order for this communication to be as efficient as possible include: the assignment of staff from both the purchaser and supplier's side; methods for agreeing to requirements changes; the documentation of changes; and the establishment of a requirements change audit trail.

4.8 PROBLEMS

The problems which are encountered if this part of the standard is not adhered to are:

- A contract will be signed for a system which the software supplier cannot deliver without either losing money or compromising on quality.
- Risks will occur which will either result in the software supplier losing money or having to sacrifice quality in order to make a profit.
- Changes to the requirements specification or statement of requirements are not noted and tracked, leading to the eventual development of a system which does not satisfy user requirements.
- A bid is made for a project which, based on faulty initial costing, leads the supplier to either lose money or compromise on quality.
- Because of the absence of standards and procedures for technical feasibility analysis a system is contracted which does not meet a constraint or set of constraints. Such systems are often seriously deficient and give rise to legal proceedings. A good example is the system which is deficient in response time, where the supplier was unaware until the later stages of the project of this deficiency.
- Project bids are so poorly structured that the company loses many contracts which it had a good chance of gaining.

4.9 CHECKS

- The quality system provides facilities, via standards, procedures and guidelines for project-specific feasibility investigation.
- Standards and procedures exist for technical feasibility investigation.
- The quality system addresses the execution of tasks which make up the process of outline project planning.
- Standards and procedures exist for outline requirements analysis and design specific to the bidding process.
- Standards and procedures exist for pre-bidding costing and the process of checking this cost.
- Standards and procedures exist for pre-bidding risk analysis.
- The quality manual provides directions for establishing a pre-development audit trail and contains standards and procedures for maintaining the trail. For example, staff are able to track the changes in the requirements specification which occurred during the process of establishing a requirements specification from a statement of requirements.
- Standards exist which describe the layout of those core aspects of bidding documents which will not vary from project to project.
- Procedures are in place for the review of bidding documentation.
- Procedures exist for the review of the contract between the supplier and the purchaser.

5

DESIGN CONTROL

5.1 INTRODUCTION

This is one of the most important parts of the ISO 9001 standard for software suppliers. It is to do with the relationship between the purchaser's requirements and the design of the system which is intended to implement these requirements. It is not totally clear in the standard which section concerns the requirements specification. I have seen interpretations of the standard which state that the requirements specification is a part of contract review—a topic detailed in the preceding chapter. However, the implication of Section 4.4.3 of ISO 9001:

> Design input requirements relating to the product shall be identified, documented and their selection reviewed by the supplier for adequacy.

seems to indicate that this section is the one which guides requirements documentation and validation. However, I have seen other interpretations which include it under the topic of design control. The question of what section of the ISO 9001 standard is relevant to the requirements specification is an academic one; the important point is that it should be addressed. In this book I shall deal with it in this chapter, although I would not argue with anyone who tells you it is really part of contract review.

5.2 STANDARDS AND PROCEDURES FOR DESIGN AND REQUIREMENTS

A major concern of this part of the standard is that the supplier should have standards and procedures which control and verify the design of the software system in order to ensure that the purchaser's requirements are met. The most naked indication of this can be found in Section 4.4.1 of ISO 9001:

The supplier shall establish and maintain procedures to control and verify the design of the product in order to ensure that the specified requirements are met.

There are a number of implications in this statement. The first is that there should be a standard for the requirements specification and a standard for the system design, together with procedures which govern the development of both these vital documents. The standard for the requirements specification should detail how the document is structured: normally this means partitioning the document into a number of sections. One major section will deal with the functionality of the system; another section will deal with the inherent data in the system; other sections would deal with other system properties such as response time, reliability, interfaces with other systems, the target computer, limits on file size and memory occupancy, and resilience.

Since the functional specification—what the system should do—is the important part of the requirements specification the standard for this document should instruct analysts to build some structure into this section of the requirements specification. Normally, this means that the functional specification will be hierarchic: functions are expressed in terms of subfunctions which, in turn, are expressed in terms of sub-subfunctions, and so on. In this way the communication with the purchaser will be easier; for example, communication on large projects is rarely with one member of a purchaser's staff, but with staff who might be responsible for one functional area. By structuring a functional specification hierarchically the supplier ensures that details of functions irrelevant to a member of the purchaser's staff do not intrude upon that member of staff's reading of the functional specification.

For management information systems, and some real-time applications such as command and control, the data which is manipulated by a system will be very large. The supplier must have standards which govern the specification of this data. It is worth stressing that this specification would be logical not physical, i.e. implementation details will not intrude. For example, at this stage of the project the way the data is stored, say in an indexed sequential file, should not be specified. All that is required is to list the main entities in the system, their attributes and their relationship with other entities in the system. For example, in an air-traffic control system an important entity is the plane: it would have a number of attributes including its flight number, destination and current position, and would be related to an entity such as an air-traffic controller by virtue of the fact that a particular controller would be responsible for the safety of a number of planes within the airspace he or she controls.

As well as standards and procedures for requirements specification, there should be standards and procedures for design.

Design can be split into two parts: system design and detailed design. The former concerns the development and specification of an architecture in terms of chunks of software which this book will call *modules*—for the reader used to third-generation languages a module will be a subroutine, while for a reader used to fourth-generation languages a module will be a program which would normally implement some transaction. System design also addresses the development of a data architecture which specifies how the data is to be implemented in terms of variables, files, tables, etc.

Detailed design is the process of filling out the details within a system design. Typically a system design standard would insist that the designer specifies the function of each module in a system using some notation—normally natural language. The aim of detailed design is to examine each module specification and describe the processing that occurs in each module in terms of a program design language. In a third-generation environment program design languages look very much like a programming language, with the normal control constructs that you would expect in languages such as C and Pascal. However, the detailed processing within these control constructs is usually specified in natural language. In a fourth-generation environment where the concept of a control structure does not hold, the program design language will mirror the query processing that occurs in fourth-generation languages. It is important to point out that most suppliers tend to only carry out system design, and omit detailed design, preferring to transform the system design into program code directly. Normally it is only suppliers who are worried about portability who employ detailed design. There is no problem *vis-à-vis* ISO 9001 over not using a detailed design notation, as the standard is not prescriptive about this level of detail. However, the important point is that if you employ a detailed design notation then there must be a standard for it.

Tips and techniques 10

One useful notation for specifying a system design in a third-generation language is known as a *module interconnection language*. This just consists of a notation which describes what each module does, what its interface with the world is, what modules call it and what modules it calls. Such a notation can be cleverly designed in such a way that a simple tool can take a module description, and convert it into a code skeleton into which a programmer inserts program code with information such as the functionality of the module copied in as a comment. An example of a module description expressed in such a language is:

%%%%
Module Update
Parameters DesData, Flag
Global variables affected Status
Calls BringIn
Called by Main, SensorCheck, SensorOut, SensorIn, SystemStatus
Function The function of this module is to examine the data within the array *DesData* and check if any of the items in the array are out of the current range. If they are, then the parameter *Flag* is set to true, otherwise it is set to false. If the system status is normal then the global variable *Status* is set to true.
%%%%

Other information could of course be included in such a notation. For example, if the notation was used to express the design of information systems, then the screens associated with the module would be mentioned.

One of the most important sections of this part of the ISO 9001 standard states that the output from the design process:

	A	B	C	D
1	x		x	x
2		x	x	
3	x		x	x
4	x	x	x	
5	x			x

Table 5.1 A verification matrix

shall be documented and expressed in terms of requirements, calculations and analyses.

This states that at the end of the design phase the supplier should have documented the design, provided documentation that the design meets the purchaser's functional requirements and provided evidence that non-functional attributes such as memory size and response time, which may be detailed in the requirements specification, have been met by the design. I regard this as the key statement in this section of the standard. Get this right in your quality system and you can assume that you stand a good chance of passing ISO 9001 on design control.

5.3 TRACEABILITY

An important concept implied by this part of the standard is *functional traceability*. What this term means is that it should be possible to trace from a function in the requirements specification to the modules which implement it. For example, a quality system which is of an ISO 9001 standard should enable someone to look at the functional specification part of the requirements specification and the system design, and quickly identify which modules will be executed when a particular function is exercised. A good quality system should also support traceability in the opposite direction; that is, someone can examine the system design, pinpoint a module, and quickly detail the functions in the functional specification which that module helps to implement.

Traceability is vitally important for a number of reasons connected with validation and maintenance. It is worth examining two examples before proceeding to the next section. The first example involves validation. The next section of this chapter stresses the validation of a design with respect to the requirements specification, that is, the question of whether a design correctly implements the properties described in the requirements specification. A major part of the validation process involves checking that the functions in the functional specification part of the requirements specification are implemented in the system design. If it is possible to trace from a function to the modules that implement it, then this process would be quite easy, not too time consuming and would not be error-prone.

Another example where traceability helps development is during regression testing: the testing of a system during maintenance. A major activity during software maintenance is the modification of modules in response to events such as errors being notified, or requirements changes being generated. Let us assume that a purchaser asks for a requirements change in a function which necessitates changes to some of the modules in the system. After the changes have occurred, there is a need to not only retest the function that has been modified, but also any functions which invoke the modules that have been modified. The reason for this is that in modifying the modules in response to an event such as a requirements change, the programmer who carried out the modifications could have altered other functions which should have remained unchanged. Traceability enables development staff to detect which functions need to be retested quickly.

Tips and techniques 11

One of the most useful methods for documenting traceability is the *verification matrix*. This consists of a table whose columns represent the modules in a system and whose rows represent functions which are detailed in the requirements specification. An example of such a table is shown on the previous page as Table 5.1. This shows the verification matrix for a small system which only consists of four modules and whose requirements specification only details five functions. Each row documents the fact that a particular set of modules will be executed when a particular function is exercised. For example, the third row shows that when function 3 is exercised modules A, C and D will be executed. This matrix is developed by the design team after the system design has been completed. It serves two purposes: it is a quality record which provides assurance that the functional properties of the system are implemented by the system design and it also provides traceability documentation.

5.4 VALIDATION

A major implication of this part of the ISO 9001 standard is that standards and procedures should be in place which help development staff check that a design meets its requirements specification. Section 4.4.5 of the standard states that:

> Design verification shall establish that design output meets the design input requirements (see 4.4.4) by means of design control measures ....

This validation should not only cover functional correctness, but should include all the other properties of the system such as file size, memory occupancy and response time. It is worth issuing a warning here: validation of some properties such as response time can be very difficult and is not an exact science. Even so, the quality system should provide facilities whereby the confidence of the supplier is increased that the system meets its requirements. For example, there really is no scientific theory which enables staff to predict accurately the response time of complex concurrent real-time systems. However, the quality system should provide facilities such as technical reviews which might, for example, examine the system architecture and compare it with similar architectures of systems which have been developed in the past and for which response time is known, in order to increase the supplier's confidence that response time will be close enough to that specified in the requirements specification for the purchaser to be happy—or at least close enough that simple optimization will bring the response time within an acceptable distance of that specified by the purchaser.

There are a number of activities which can be used to validate a system design against a requirements specification. The main one is the technical review. Part of a procedure for running a design review is:

7 Technical reviews

One of the main techniques that we use to implement quality control is the technical review. This is just a meeting of staff who examine a critical project document for correctness and who issue a report on the problems that have been encountered during the review. The process of organizing a review is shown below.

The member of staff responsible for an item that is to be reviewed informs the chair of the review that the item is ready. The chair checks that the item is in a fit state for review. If is it not, then it is returned to the originator for reworking. If the item is ready for review the chair books a room, selects the participants for the review—usually between three and five members of staff—arranges for the review material and any supporting material to be duplicated and sent to the participants, and informs each participant of the date and place of the review. Who the chair invites to the review depends on the material to be reviewed, as does the nature of the supporting material. These details can be found in Sections 7.1 to 7.8 which contain details that are specific to a review type.

For many of our reviews there will be checklists which describe the particular problems that review participants should be looking for. Copies of the checklists should also be sent to each participant. The review is held. One of the participants is nominated as a recorder. The chair will normally ask any of the participants whether there are any general problems with the item that is being reviewed. After this, the document is processed serially, item by item. For example, if it is a requirements specification this will be done on a paragraph by paragraph basis; if it is program code then it will be done on a module by module basis. Each time a problem is discovered it is noted down on the review report form. This form contains sections which contain a description of the problems, where they occur, the staff member responsible and the severity of the error. For further details of this form see Section 8.1.

At the end of the review the chair will decide whether the item has passed the review, has passed subject to minor revision or has not passed. In the first case the chair signs the object off on the review report form. In the second case the originator of the item rectifies the minor problem and the chair of the review checks the changes and signs the review report form off. In the third case a re-review is needed.

Once an item has been succesfully reviewed it should be consigned to the project library accompanied by the review report form. The remainder of this section describes information specific to each review type that our quality manual supports.

7.1 The design specification review

There should normally be either four or five participants at this review, one of whom should not be the project manager or the manager to whom the author of the item to be reviewed reports. For this review the following staff should be invited: the author of the section of design that is to be reviewed, a designer from another project, one of the system test team and staff charged with implementing the system design including at least one senior programmer.

The documentation items that are provided with this review are the section of design specification that is to be reviewed and the section of the requirements specification which the design implements. These items should be circulated to the participants. A document that should also be made available for reference during the review is the journal which records the interaction between the company and the customer; the bulk of this document precludes it being copied and circulated to the participants of the review. If a scenario analysis has been carried out then any scenarios should be made available to the participants.

The checklist which is relevant to this review is checklist RR 1.2, with which all participants should be provided.

A design review is a meeting of staff who examine the design and the requirements specification and attempt to detect errors. There should be standards and procedures in existence which determine: the conduct of such reviews; who should attend; what documents are to be reviewed; how factors such as functionality, response time and memory occupancy are validated; the format of any documentation which lists errors detected; and the role of the purchaser in such reviews. When a company develops large systems a number of technical reviews specific to a particular property of the system will normally be held. For example, there may be a technical review or series of reviews which examine sizing issues. If the company organizes its reviews in such a way, then there should be separate standards and procedures for each type of review, although there will be much commonality between these standards and procedures.

Reviews are not the only way of validating a system. An increasingly important technique is prototyping: the generation of an early version of a system in order to check out the functionality of a system. If a company uses prototyping, then the quality system should provide direction about this activity: the type of prototyping to be used, the methods used to elicit feedback from the purchaser, the aim of the prototyping exercise and communication with the purchaser during prototyping. There are also a number of other techniques, such as simulation and walkthroughs, which can be used for validation. If they are used, then the quality system should address them in terms of standards and procedures.

5.5 ORGANIZATIONAL INTERFACES

Another important feature of this subsection of the ISO 9001 standard is the specification that the organizational and technical interfaces between different groups shall be identified and their interface documented. This is a reference to the provision in the quality manual of details of how the relationship between the software development team and other agencies such as hardware suppliers should be managed. It should also detail the relationship between the design teams who are designing subsystems and how the relationship between the analysts and the designers on the project is handled. The quality system should document the means of communication, the standards for the document used for communication and aspects such as the querying of the functional properties of the system by the designers. If there is any need for liaison between the designers and the purchaser, this should also be the subject of standards and procedures.

5.6 DESIGN INPUT REQUIREMENTS

Another part of the standard specifies that design input requirements relating to the system to be developed shall be identified and documented, and that poorly specified requirements shall be resolved with staff who drew them up. This is a reference to the fact that the requirements specification, which is the main input into the design process, should accurately reflect the purchaser requirements which were initially detailed in some statement of requirements. The implication here is that there should be adequately specified communication routes between the design team and the analysts who drew up the requirements specification, so that queries and problems with the requirements specification are settled easily and efficiently. These communication routes should be specified in either the project plan or the quality plan.

5.7 CONFIGURATION MANAGEMENT

A final part of this section of the standard states that all changes should be documented, reviewed, applied, checked and that any related documents which also need to be changed are processed correctly:

> The supplier shall establish and maintain procedures for the identification, documentation and appropriate review and approval of all changes and modifications.

This is a reference to the configuration management practices adopted by the company. This topic is considered later in the book. However, it is worth saying here that a company which has an ISO 9001-certified configuration management system should have standards and procedures for: initiating change; having the change considered by some body which decides on whether it is to be allowed or rejected; communicating the change to staff charged with implementing it; updating documentation to reflect the change; informing staff such as analysts and designers that documents have been changed; and validating a change to ensure that other changes which were not sanctioned have not been applied.

5.8 RELATION TO ISO 9000-3

Sections 5.3, 5.4, 5.5, 5.6, 5.7 and 6.1 of ISO 9000-3 are relevant to this part of the ISO 9001 standard. Section 5.3 describes the process whereby a purchaser's requirements specification is built up in consultation with the supplier. It also describes the important principle that the development of the requirements specification should occur in as smooth a way as possible, for example by nominating each side's representatives well in advance of the process of requirements elicitation and specification. This section also outlines the principle that change control should be implemented early in a software project. An important point made is that the purchaser's requirements:

> should be stated precisely enough so as to allow validation during product acceptance.

Section 5.4 of ISO 9000-3 is about planning. The implication of this part of the standard is that: all activities which make up the requirements analysis and specification process should be identified and documented; the lines of communication between the purchaser and supplier should be specified; and assumptions about the requirements analysis process, such as the fact that the customer will read and send in comments on the requirements specification within a specified period, should be documented in the project plan.

    Section 5.5 is about quality planning and the quality plan for a project. The important point made here, relevant to the requirements analysis and design processes, is that a project at the end of the design phase should generate evidence that the design produced by the project's staff meets the purchaser's requirements, as detailed in the requirements specification, and that quality records exist which demonstrate this, for example minutes of technical reviews which have been signed off by the chairs of the reviews.

Section 5.6 is about design and implementation. The relevance of this section lies in the fact that it details that a proper design method should be used, that design standards should be employed and that design considerations such as memory occupancy should be brought to the attention of the designers.

Section 5.7 is about testing and validation. The important points here are that proper planning for testing should take place, that the system and acceptance tests should be generated from the requirements specification and that validation of the design against the requirements specification should take place—usually via a technical review.

Section 6.1 describes configuration management. The important point to make here is that both the design and the requirements specification should come under configuration control in a project. Once these documents have been baselined or frozen, any changes to them have to be considered formally. Proposed changes have to be documented, evaluated by a change control board, change documentation generated, changes implemented, the changes validated and new versions of the specifications distributed to relevant staff.

5.9 PROBLEMS

The problems which are encountered if this part of the standard is not adhered to are:

- A poorly expressed requirements specification which gives rise to an incorrect design, system test specification, program code and user documentation.
- A poorly constructed design which does not match user functions and gives rise to program code which is in error.
- A design which does not implement non-functional attributes such as response time adequately.
- Poorly specified modules which give rise to program code which is in error, or at least wastes programmer time when the module specification is queried.
- Poor correspondence between a design and a requirements specification which results in more resources than is necessary being spent on validation and reworking.
- Poor correspondence between a design and a requirements specification which results in more resources than is necessary being spent on maintenance.
- Inadequate standards for functional validation resulting in errors slipping through, and only being detected at the later stages of software development such as system testing. The detection and rectification of errors at such a late stage in a project is much more expensive than if the errors were detected close to the point when they were committed.
- Inadequate standards for non-functional validation. This leads, at best, to unnecessary, major reworking during the later stages of a project. At worst, it can lead to the delivery of unusable systems.
- Poorly specified interfaces between the design team and other parts of the project, for example the staff charged with requirements analysis. There are two results of this: first, unnecessary effort is spent in communication; and second, errors are committed in the inadequate, informal communication channels that will be used if a formal communication channel is not set up.

- Inadequate change control, leading to designs which are out of step with the requirements specification. This leads to the development of program code, user documentation and system tests which are out of step with purchaser requirements.

5.10 CHECKS

- Standards and procedures exist which describe the process of constructing the requirements specification and matching it up with the purchaser's statement of requirements.
- Standards exist which describe the form and structure of the requirements specification and the system design. If the supplier uses a detailed design notation, then a standard should exist for this too.
- Standards and procedures exist which detail all the validation activities that a supplier uses to validate a design against a requirements specification. These activities will include prototyping, technical reviews, the calculation of response time, the calculation of file occupancy figures and simulation.
- Planning standards and procedures insist that adequate communication channels are set up between designers, analysts and the purchaser. These channels should be documented in the project plan.
- Design and requirements specification standards insist that there is a traceability between functions expressed in the latter and the modules specified in the former.
- Adequate change control procedures are in existence, and the system design specification and requirements specification are expected to conform to these procedures.

6

DOCUMENT CONTROL

6.1 INTRODUCTION

A modern software project generates many different types of documents. The main documents are feasibility reports, project plans, requirements specifications, system designs, detailed designs, systems test specifications and acceptance test specifications. Also, these documents will exist in a number of versions. This part of the standard is concerned with ensuring that project documents must be adequate when they are released, and that the process of controlling change in a software project—the discipline known as *configuration management*—is carried out efficiently and correctly.

6.2 CONFIGURATION ITEMS

A common way of ensuring that change is carried out efficiently is by means of the establishment of baselines and configuration items. A *configuration item* is normally an important document in a project or some collection of source code such as the modules which make up a subsystem. Typical configuration items include the requirements specification, the user manual, the system design and the program code of a subsystem. In a large project it is normally the practice to designate documents at the subsystem level as configuration items, for example the system design of a subsystem.

A *baseline* is a version of a document which has been placed under control of a configuration management system that has been set up for a project. Up to the point that a configuration item has been baselined changes can occur in any way, without any control being applied. However, once a configuration item has been baselined all change is rigorously controlled. This is the subject of another section of this chapter. However, it is worth stating here that a quality system should provide guidance to the project manager on the identification of configuration items and their specification in the project plan.

An important part of this requirement of the standard is that before a document or a chunk of program code has been baselined adequate quality control documentation should be in existence which enables the project manager to decide whether it is ready for baselining. For example, in making the decision whether to baseline a requirements specification a project manager will need to examine the validation records which are relevant to this document. Normally a requirements specification is validated by a series of technical reviews which check that it corresponds to user requirements. These meetings will give rise to problems or errors which are then cleared up by the analyst who has produced the part of the requirements specification which has been reviewed. The quality system should provide standards which enable the project manager to determine quickly that all the problems which have been detected by requirements reviews have been dealt with, and that all of the requirements specification has been reviewed. Once the project manager is happy with this, he or she can indicate that the requirements specification is baselined.

Baselining is normally achieved in two ways. First, by adding the document name to a document or file which describes the current system configuration. It is important that this document or file is readily available to any member of a project so that they do not work with out-of-date configuration items. The other, more important, way to indicate that a document has been baselined is to alter its numbering. For example, one practice which is frequently adopted is not to allocate a configuration item a version number until it has been baselined; prior to baselining the configuration item will only be identified by the date. After baselining the document will be given a version number.

Depending on the complexity of the system to be developed, and its size, this version number could be a single digit or two digits separated by some character such as a full stop. The first digit would represent a major version number while the second digit would represent a minor version number. In this form of numbering small changes to a version would result in the minor version number being incremented, while major changes would result in the major version number being incremented and the minor version number being reset to one.

6.3 CONFIGURATION CONTROL

Once a configuration item has been baselined a rigorous process of change control should be adopted for it. This involves changes being proposed, evaluated and then either sanctioned or refused. The standard is unambiguous on this subject:

> The supplier shall establish and maintain procedures to control all documents and data that relate to the requirements of this International Standard. These documents shall be reviewed and approved for adequacy by authorized personnel prior to issue.

The main medium for this is a function known as the *change control board*. This sounds like a group of people; however, on anything but the largest projects the functions of the change control board are normally discharged by a project manager, a senior member of the developmental staff such as a senior analyst or someone from the quality assurance function.

The process of configuration control is shown in Figure 6.1. A change to a configu-

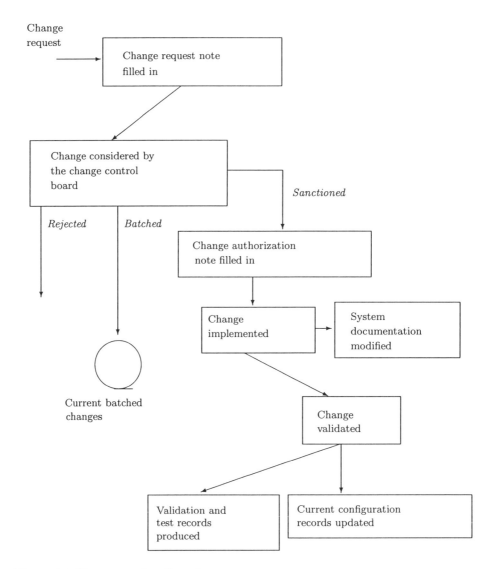

Figure 6.1 The process of configuration management

ration item can occur for a number of reasons. For example, it could be because an error was discovered in an important part of the documentation, or it could have been raised as a result of a change in user requirements. The change is submitted to the change control board for consideration.

Normally, some form of analysis of the change has been carried out by project staff, and information about the severity of the change is provided as well as a description of the change. An extract from a procedure which describes the process of notifying change is shown here (the term *configuration board* used in the extract is a synonym for change control board):

5.1 Change notification

Throughout our projects change will occur. It will occur for a number of reasons, the main ones being changes in purchaser requirements and the detection of errors by development staff. It is important that the change control process should be as visible as possible. Changes have been applied on past projects which have not been documented. They have, in one case, given rise to litigation.

The change request form which is used to notify change to the configuration board is detailed on page 45 of the quality manual. The steps for filling in this form are: first, determine the reason for the change—normally the change will have been notified to you by developmental staff or staff whose function is to liaise with the purchaser; second, determine the effect the change will have on the project, for example a change due to an error detected during programming might give rise to changes in the requirements specification, design and system test specification; third, the amount of resources required for modification of project documents and code should be determined, together with the amount of resources required to revalidate the system after the change has been applied.

After the resources have been calculated you should enter the amount on the change request form and give the change a severity rating from 1 to 5, with 1 being a trivial change and 5 being a change which would lead to major project resources being deployed. Do not forget to fill in the section marked *rationale*. This part of the form contains the rationale which led you to assign the particular severity rating that you specified. You should then fill in the final part of the form which asks you for a preliminary assessment of whether the change should be allowed by the configuration board. You should bear in mind that only trivial changes which have little resource impact or changes which reflect missing or imperfectly implemented customer requirements are normally allowed.

The reason why severity is specified is so that the change control board can decide what the result of a change request is to be. The ISO 9001 standard states that:

Changes to documents shall be reviewed and approved by the same functions/organizations that performed the original review and approval unless specifically designated otherwise. The designated organizations shall have access to pertinent background information upon which to base their review and approval.

The change control board looks at a number of factors in deciding what is to happen to a change, the main factors being the impact of the change on the software project and also whether the change is necessary in order to satisfy the requirements specification generated at the beginning of the project. There are three decisions that could be made by a change control board:

- *Allowed.* The change is to be applied as soon as possible.
- *Disallowed.* The change will not take place.
- *Batched.* The change will take place at some time in the future.

Changes which are allowed are normally those changes which the project regards as important, or which are relatively trivial. For example, a change in response to a serious error which would result in the non-implementation of an important function would come under this category, as would a minor change to the display of data requested by the purchaser.

Changes which are disallowed are those changes which the change control board agree are not necessary, impact the project to a serious degree, or fall outside the remit of the project. For example, a change request by a purchaser which would result in the addition of a function that was not initially documented in the requirements specification would come into this category. If a purchaser request has been disallowed, then the configuration management system should allow the option of the purchaser re-requesting the change. In this case the change is costed, the impact on the project in terms of extended delivery time is specified and the purchaser is asked whether he or she wishes to re-present the change, with of course the eventual outcome being delay of the project and an increase in the cost of the system being notified by the supplier. If the purchaser agrees, then the change is normally re-presented and allowed.

Changes which are delayed are those changes which the software supplier thinks are a good idea, but which, for one reason or another, cannot be immediately implemented. An example is a change to a financial package requested by a purchaser who claims that the package does not do what the manual says it should. The supplier may discover that the purchaser has misread the manual, but that the proposed change would actually make sense in marketing the package: that it provides some extra functionality that may sell more copies of the package. In this case the proposed changed is turned down as not immediately implementable, but it is placed in a queue of changes to be implemented during the development of the next major version of the package.

Tips and techniques 12

The extract from a procedure contained on page 53 contains an important principle that you should bear in mind when writing standards and procedures; that is, that whenever a member of staff makes a decision on a project which could, potentially, affect that project in terms of quality, then the quality system should insist that the member of staff has to provide a rationale for that decision. For example, when a project manager puts forward a project cost he or she should be asked to explain the basis on which the cost estimate was made and the steps that he or she employed. It is worth doing this even for low-level activities, since asking someone to explain why a certain task was carried out in a particular way actively makes them think about the task a lot more deeply. For example, your standards for module testing should insist that the programmer describes why he or she selected the test data that was used.

Once a positive change decision has been arrived at two events occur. First, the change is added to the configuration management system documentation. Second, the change is communicated to the staff who have been nominated as responsible for its implementation. The change is carried out, and all documentation associated with the change is modified and new versions of the documentation produced. For example, if a requirements change has been authorized, then a wide variety of documents will need to be modified, including the requirements specification, the system design, detailed design, program code and all the associated test documentation.

A quality system which has been certified to ISO 9001 requires a number of components to address configuration control. First, there is a need for standards for the documentation which is used to notify the change control board of a potential change. Second, there is a need for procedures which help the project manager establish clear lines of communication between staff raising changes and the change control board. These should be specified in the project plan. Third, there is a need for a procedure which details how a typical change control board will operate. Fourth, there is a need for a standard which describes the results of the change appraisal process carried out by the board. Fifth, there is a need for a standard which describes the numbering to be used to identify versions of a configuration item; usually this would be a version number and a date with an associated list of previous version numbers together with their date of issue on the cover page of the configuration item. Sixth, there is a need for a standard which describes how a sanctioned change is communicated to staff who are to carry out the change. Finally, there is a need for validation after a change has been applied.

6.4 CHANGE VALIDATION

Once a change has taken place there is a need for it to be validated. This validation could take a number of forms depending on the severity of the change. A small change, for example a modification to the program code of a single module, would only require the generation of some module test data and the rerunning of any affected system tests; a large requirements change would require a number of reviews to take place together with the generation of new module test data, integration test data, system test data and acceptance test data.

A quality system certified to ISO 9001 should have standards and procedures which govern the process of validating a change. These should ensure that adequate records are produced which show that the change has been carried out and checked, and that only the change sanctioned by the change control board has been applied. As an example of this consider a change in requirements which resulted in further changes in the design, program code and system tests for a system. Normally this size of change might be reviewed and signed-off by a meeting between the project staff responsible for the change and a senior member of the project such as a senior designer.

At this meeting, the staff responsible for the change would show how the changes were applied, with the steps taken to check the change together with their associated quality records, and provide evidence that the change did not affect those parts of the system which should have remained unaffected. The senior member of staff would then look at the new version of the documentation which incorporates the change and check that no other modifications have occurred—something normally achieved by the quality manual insisting on the use of change bars in any modified document. If the member of staff was happy with the changes, then he or she signs them off and the version numbers of the configuration items affected by the changes are then modified.

6.5 STATUS ACCOUNTING

There is a need for the current status of a system to be documented. This is quite clearly stated by the standard:

> A master list or equivalent document control procedure shall be established to identify the current revision of documents in order to preclude the use of non-applicable documents.

This means that the quality system should provide a standard which describes the status of a system in terms of those configuration items which have been baselined together with their version numbers. For software suppliers who produce packages which can be tailored to individual purchasers' requirements this documentation will be extensive, but for the suppliers of bespoke software it is often no more than a list of configuration items that have been baselined, their current version number, the date when the current version was produced and a list of previous versions. The aim of this status documentation is to ensure that the probability that staff will use out-of-date documentation will be small.

6.6 RELATION TO ISO 9000-3

The relevant sections of ISO 9000-3 are 6.1 and 6.2. Section 6.1 details the fact that a configuration management system should be used by the supplier. This configuration management system should identify configuration items, keep track of versions of a system, control the concurrent updating of a system and provide standards and procedures which enable change to be tracked from the initial change notification to the point where new versions of documents and code are released.

Section 6.1.2 imposes the requirement that the software supplier should develop a configuration management plan which specifies the flow of change data and information, the responsibilities of staff for configuration activities, the tools and techniques to be used for configuration management and the points in a software project when individual items are brought under configuration control.

Section 6.1.3 reiterates many of the principles described in this chapter: that configuration items should be identified, that version information is kept and that traceability is maintained between the original statement of requirements generated by the purchaser and the software:

> The identification of a software item should be handled in such a way that the relationship between the item and the contract requirements can be demonstrated.

Section 6.1.3 also describes the fact that procedures should be in existence which handle the process of receiving, evaluating, issuing and validating changes to a system.

Section 6.2 of ISO 9000-3 is about the documents that are generated during a software project. This includes technical documents such as the requirements specification, the system design and the system test plan, but also planning documents. It states that all documents should be validated before they are released to staff for use. For example, the system design should be reviewed by a series of technical reviews before it is given to programmers for implementation. It also makes the point that all documents should be up to date and all obsolete documents should be withdrawn. It reminds the reader that if documents are held on computer files, then special attention should be paid to the access, distribution and archiving of these documents.

6.7 PROBLEMS

The problems which are encountered if this part of the standard is not adhered to are:

- Developmental staff use documents which are out of date and, consequently, will develop systems which do not match purchaser requirements or do not match the system's design.
- Developmental staff spend needless time chasing up the right version of a document or chunk of program code.
- Changes to a system are applied haphazardly and are not documented. This either results in a system which does not meet its requirements or the expenditure of large amounts of extra resource in order to ensure that it does.
- Changes to a system cause errors in other parts of the system which should have remained unchanged. This leads to systems which are very error-prone.
- Staff apply unsanctioned changes to a system. This often leads to the development of error-prone software.

6.8 CHECKS

- The quality manual offers guidance to the project manager about the identification of configuration items.
- The quality manual contains a standard for describing configuration items in the project plan.
- The quality manual contains a procedure which describes the steps necessary for developing a configuration management system for a particular project, together with a standard which describes how this system is described in the project plan or the quality plan.
- A procedure exists in the quality manual which details how the communication channels between the change control board and staff involved in development or servicing are set up and maintained.
- A standard exists for the documentation that is sent to the change control board describing a proposed change.
- A procedure exists which details how the change control board organizes its business.
- A standard exists which details how the results of a change control board decision, or set of decisions, is communicated to developmental staff.
- A procedure exists which governs the process of carrying out a change sanctioned by the change control board and validating that change.
- A procedure exists which describes how the application of a change and its validation is checked and signed off.
- A standard exists which describes how the current configuration of a system is expressed in terms of its current configuration items and their versions.

7

PURCHASING

7.1 INTRODUCTION

This section details the issues a quality system needs to address when software projects have to purchase or use external products—either software or hardware. These external products could either be subcontracted or could be provided by an external agency such as the purchaser or a government department. It describes what a software supplier should do to ensure that these external products have the same level of quality as the software that will incorporate them.

7.2 SUBCONTRACTED REQUIREMENTS

A major implication of this part of the standard is that when software is to be purchased by the supplier, and produced by a subcontractor, the supplier should specify the software requirements at the same level of detail that is used on the project that employs the software. If not, then the contracted software will be a weak link. In effect there should be standards and procedures which tell the software supplier how he or she will behave with respect to the subcontractor. This behaviour should be indistinguishable from the behaviour that the supplier expects from the purchaser for the software: that is, that a proper contract is drawn up which deals with entities such as milestones, deliverables and requirements, with the supplier closely monitoring the work of the subcontractor in the same way that the purchaser monitors the supplier's work.

One area where this part of the standard impacts the supplier is in the production of the requirements specification. The same standard used for the expression of the requirements of the software developed in-house should be used by the staff who are specifying the requirements for any subcontracted software. The only difference is that the task of specifying this part of the system may be carried out earlier than the task of specifying the remainder of the system requirements. The reason for this is that software subcontracting is always seen as something of a risk, and suppliers are normally keen to allow as much time as possible for the development of subcontracted software. Also, the purchaser will normally want to review all requirements specifications and the process is much easier if the specifications generated for a project and for subcontracted software are developed using similar standards:

> The supplier shall review and approve purchasing documents for adequacy of specified requirements prior to release.

Another area where this part of the standard impacts is the development of the system and acceptance tests. When the requirements specification has been baselined the supplier will generate the system and acceptance tests in outline. At this stage of the project it is important that the tests generated for the part of the system which is to be subcontracted should be indistinguishable from those generated for the part of the system which is to be produced by the supplier. It could be that the outline tests for the subcontracted software might be generated first, in order to allow for possible problems with a subcontractor; however, the important point is that these tests should be indistinguishable from those used by the supplier.

In general the precept which should be used when specifying standards and procedures for dealing with subcontracted software is: how do we want the purchaser to behave towards us? The supplier should then behave in this way towards the subcontractor.

7.3 TECHNICAL DOCUMENTATION

The model assumed for subcontracting in the previous section was of a software supplier providing a requirements specification for a subcontractor. It is by no means rare for the supplier to provide design documentation and only assume that the subcontractor will carry out programming, module testing and integration testing on the software that is being subcontracted. This is a lower risk option than that detailed in the preceding section, since the supplier is in tighter control for a proportionately longer period. However, the implication here is that the design documentation that is produced is developed using the same standards and procedures that are used to produce the part of the system for which the supplier is responsible.

Another important point that does not emerge if one assumes that the behaviour of the supplier *vis-à-vis* the subcontractor is solely that between a purchaser and supplier is the role of technical documentation. Normally the purchaser is not interested in receiving technical documentation such as system designs, integration test descriptions and module test descriptions, apart from the rare occasions when the purchaser is going to maintain the system. However, when the supplier acts as a purchaser to the subcontractor it is expected that system documentation, of the same standard as that used on the main project, is received by the supplier. It is also important that the subcontractor uses the same, or similar, standards for all the technical activities that are to be carried out, for example that the same programming standards that are adopted for the main software project are employed. This is important for maintenance of the system.

7.4 SUBCONTRACTING DECISIONS

The decision when to use subcontractors for software development is often a difficult one. Using a subcontractor implies that the profit on a project will be less than if in-house staff are used. Normally, the decision about whether to subcontract is based on a consideration of risk. For example, a project manager may decide to subcontract if he or she believes that the level of expertise for a particular task in his or her company is so low that there is either a significant risk that the software quality will be poor, or that such a large amount of resource needs to be expended on training existing staff that the overall viability of the project is threatened. A quality system should offer guidelines to the project manager which enables him or her to decide whether to subcontract or not. The quality system should also describe the procedures which should be carried out when subcontracting has been decided on. This will include procedures for issuing bid documents such as a requirements specification, the development of the technical parts of a legal contract, liaison with the purchasing function and the eventual selection of a subcontractor.

7.5 SELECTING A SUBCONTRACTOR

The ISO 9001 certified quality system should contain procedures which have to be followed when selecting a subcontractor. This point is made quite clearly in the standard:

> The supplier shall select subcontractors on the basis of their ability to meet subcontract requirements, including quality requirements. The supplier shall establish and maintain records of acceptable subcontractors (see 4.16).

> The selection of subcontractors, and the type and extent of control exercised by the supplier, shall be dependent upon the type of product and, where appropriate, on records of a subcontractor's previously demonstrated capability or performance.

These would mainly include evaluation procedures. They would involve a selection of activities: asking the software developer to fill in a questionnaire on developmental and quality assurance practices, visiting the software developer in order to ask a number of tough technical questions, examining past project records where a potential subcontractor has been involved, telephoning companies who have previously used the potential subcontractor and carrying out financial investigations into the solvency of the subcontractor. Procedures can never govern the actual selection of a subcontractor: they only provide direction on information gathering. Nevertheless, a good quality system should provide guidelines which help the project manager decide on which subcontractor to use.

Many of these actions may already be part of a company's purchasing standards. However, I rarely find the more technical activities such as visiting a potential subcontractor and asking some tricky developmental and quality assurance-oriented questions included in such procedures; the reason for this is that these procedures tend to be generic and oriented toward the purchasing of a wide variety of artefacts, ranging from bolts to cranes.

One of the most valuable inputs into the process of selecting a subcontractor is an appraisal of their previous performance. This means that, as part of the standards and procedures which govern project debriefing meetings, there should be an instruction to the project manager in charge of the debriefed project to produce a candid assessment of the performance of any subcontractor that was used.

Tips and techniques 13

A quick way to evaluate a subcontractor is to ask for the agendas of board meetings held over the last two or three years together with the minutes of any discussions on software quality. If there are no quality discussions, then that is a poor sign. If there are some discussions, but they are scheduled near to the end of the meeting, that is a slightly better sign, but not ideal. If the discussions about software quality occur at the beginning of a board meeting, and are primarily about prevention and improvement, then that is an excellent sign.

Part of a procedure for selecting subcontractors is:

23 Subcontractor evaluation

Occasionally we use subcontractors for software development. Normally these subcontractors are used when we do not have enough experience with a particular programming language or computer. Care has to be taken over the selection of such contractors. It is important that the subcontractor(s) chosen for a project develop software which is at least to the quality of the software that your project is to deliver. The following actions and checks need to be carried out:

1. Check that the contractor is certified to an external standard such as BS5750; certainly, if the subcontractor has achieved BS5750, then there should be little need to carry out further checks on technical capability. There is still a need, however, to carry out financial checks. If no certification has been achieved, then further questions need to be asked. These are detailed below.
2. Check that any of our projects which have used the subcontractor have been happy with performance. Details for each project can be found in the project debrief file for each project. This file should contain a completed questionnaire on subcontractor performance.
3. Ask the software contractor for the names of at least two companies who you can approach to ask about performance. A subcontractor's reluctance to give such names should be regarded seriously. However, you should recognize that there may be circumstances which prevent the subcontractor giving this information; for example, it may need clearance from an agency, such as the Ministry of Defence, which is not forthcoming. If possible you should ask for more than two companies and randomly nominate two of them.
4. Apply the checklist found in Appendix B.1 of the quality manual. This will normally require a day visit to the software developer's premises. This checklist contains twenty-five questions designed to probe a software developer's technical and managerial practices. Poor answers to more than ten of these questions should be regarded seriously.
5. If the subcontractor is carrying out a large proportion of work on a project—more than 25% of the monetary worth—then a financial check should be carried out to ensure that the company is in good health. The body that carries out this check for us is *Information Systems and Intelligence*, who provide very accurate company financial profiles and are able to pronounce on the financial health of a wide variety of developers.

7.6 PURCHASED PRODUCT

A major implication in this part of the ISO 9001 standard concerns software which is purchased by the supplier. Such software can include special-purpose compilers, testing tools and spreadsheet systems. Such software is normally used in two ways. First the software may be a component of a developed system; for example, a spreadsheet may be used in order to produce charts from some stored data calculated by a system. Second, the software may be used in the development of a system; for example, a special-purpose testing tool may be used for module testing.

In both cases there is a requirement on the software supplier to have checked to see whether the software that is used will be of the same standard as that employed in the system. This is quite a tricky task to carry out since the software that is to be incorporated might vary from a package which has tens of thousands of customers to a tool which may only have received limited use.

The quality system should offer guidance to the project manager about the level of validation that a piece of purchased software should have. This level of validation will depend on two factors: the amount of previous use that the software has had and the degree of criticality of the system that is to be developed. For example, a spreadsheet system such as Lotus 1-2-3 incorporated in a simple clerical application would receive little, if any, validation. All that would be required is for the project manager to note his or her reason for not carrying out validation in the project's documentation—usually the project plan. However, a compiler used in an ultra-safety critical system, such as a nuclear power control system, would be the subject of extensive validation which would involve the supplier examining the generated program code from a number of test programs.

Usually the validation of purchased product is carried out by executing a series of system tests. These tests are normally generated from the requirements specification of the product or, more likely, the user manual. One problem that the quality system should address in connection with this validation is what to do if the documentation used to generate these tests is inadequate. This topic is dealt with in the next chapter, which deals with the specific case of software product which is provided by the purchaser.

7.7 VERIFICATION OF PURCHASED PRODUCT

Another component of the standard concerns the means by which the purchaser checks that any purchased or subcontracted software is of the same quality as that produced by the project which employs that software:

> Where specified in the contract, the purchaser or his representative shall be afforded the right to verify at source or upon receipt that purchased product conforms to specified requirements. Verification by the purchaser shall not absolve the supplier of the responsibility to provide acceptable product nor shall it preclude subsequent rejection.

Normally what adherence to this part of the standard entails is that the supplier carries out the checks on purchased software as the purchaser's representative and that test records are made available to the purchaser.

7.8 PURCHASED PRODUCT IDENTIFICATION

This part of the standard also deals with the identification of product which is to be purchased. This is normally taken to be a directive to the software supplier to specify any subcontracted software correctly and to ensure that adequate change control applies to this software as much as to the software and documentation produced in the project.

It is not mandatory for a subcontractor to use the same configuration management system as the supplier. However, the supplier should have been satisfied that the configuration system used by the subcontractor is as good as that used by the supplier. Also, the interface between the supplier's configuration management system and that used by the subcontractor should be precisely defined.

There is also an implication that the standards used for identifying program code or documentation such as a subsystem design should enable it to be easily identifiable as having originated from a subcontractor. For example, the comments used in a module should specify the name of the original programmer, together with information about the department he or she works for, or the name of the subcontractor that he or she is employed by. This rule about identification should hold for program code and all the documentation which could be produced by a subcontractor.

7.9 RELATION TO ISO 9000-3

The relevant part of ISO 9000-3 is Section 6.7. This lays down the principle that the supplier should ensure that purchased software or hardware conforms to requirements. It also reiterates the principle that the supplier will often need to validate purchased or subcontracted software by carrying out activities such as technical reviews and acceptance testing similar to those activities used for the development of the system into which purchased product is to be incorporated. A very important point implied by ISO 9000-3 is that just because a supplier may carry out validation activities such as acceptance testing, this does not absolve the supplier from ensuring that a subcontractor uses an acceptable quality system.

7.10 PROBLEMS

The problems which are encountered if this part of the standard is not adhered to are:

- Faulty software components are incorporated into a system. These either contain errors and are of poor quality, or give rise to a large amount of resource expenditure when the supplier rectifies the errors.
- Standards and procedures are used by a subcontractor which might be adequate for development but which provide problems for maintenance staff who may have to maintain a system that is expressed in two notations: the supplier's and the purchaser's.
- Poor requirements specifications are produced by a subcontractor, resulting either in poor quality software or software on which large amounts of resource are expended in order to bring the quality to acceptable levels.

- Inadequate monitoring of a subcontractor's developmental progress, leading to missed delivery dates and a subsequent slipping of developmental schedules.
- Poor system and acceptance tests are specified for subcontracted software leading to error-prone software being incorporated into a system.
- Inadequate technical documentation is produced by a software subcontractor leading to increased resources being required for maintenance of the system into which the contracted software is to be inserted.
- A poor selection of subcontractor leading to the development of poor quality contracted software.
- Poor quality product is purchased. Since the supplier has little control over bought-in software, such as a spreadsheet package, this leads to a serious degradation of software quality which cannot usually be rectified.
- Documents or software which are so poorly documented it is difficult to determine their origin. This leads to high levels of resource being expended when, for example, attempting to find out information required for the maintenance task.

7.11 CHECKS

- Procedures exist which instruct the project manager to insist on the employment of the same standards and procedures used in a project for the requirements specification of any subcontracted software.
- Procedures exist which instruct the project manager to insist that a subcontractor employs similar progress-reporting procedures as those used on the project which uses the subcontracted software.
- Procedures exist which instruct the project manager to use the same standards for the system and acceptance tests employed to judge the functional and non-functional correctness of the subcontracted software as used for validating the overall system.
- Procedures exist which instruct the project manager to insist that a subcontractor uses the same, or similar, documentation standards as those in the development of the system which is to incorporate subcontracted software.
- Procedures exist which describe the information gathering exercises that need to be carried out prior to selecting a subcontractor.
- The quality system provides guidelines which provide advice on how to select a subcontractor.
- Procedures exist which govern the interface between a project and any internal purchasing function such as a purchasing department.
- Standards and procedures for project debriefing insist that a report about subcontractor performance is produced by the project manager.
- The quality system provides guidelines which enable the project manager to decide on the level of validation that a purchased software product should receive.
- The quality system should provide standards and procedures which govern the validation that a purchased product receives. Normally these will be similar to the standards and procedures used for system and acceptance testing.
- Documentation standards for entities such as the requirements specification, system design, program modules and system tests insist that not only the staff who developed

the tests are identified, but also whether they are employed by the supplier or are staff of a subcontractor.

- The same level of configuration management practices used by the supplier are employed by a subcontractor.
- The interface between a project's configuration management system and that of the supplier's is precisely defined.

8

PURCHASER SUPPLIED PRODUCT

8.1 INTRODUCTION

This part of the standard deals with what a supplier should do when the purchaser supplies a component of a particular system or even, more rarely, software tools which aid the development. This component will normally be some software, but it can include data and hardware. In the spirit of this book this chapter will deal with the first two:

> The supplier shall establish and maintain procedures for verification, storage and maintenance of purchaser supplied product provided for incorporation into the supplies. Any such product that is lost, damaged or is otherwise unsuitable for use shall be recorded and reported to the purchaser.

The standard also makes the important point that even if the supplier claims to have checked any supplied software, this does not 'absolve the purchaser of the responsibility to provide acceptable product'. The implication here is that even if the supplier is confident about the quality of the software that he or she is providing, some checking needs to be carried out by the supplier. Some of the software-related items which can be handed over by a purchaser are:

- Software modules which may have been previously written for another system which the purchaser feels will be useful for the system that is to be developed.
- Tools used for the development of a previous system that the purchaser may feel will be useful in the development of a current system.
- Files of test data used for activities such as performance testing.
- Documentation such as requirements specifications, system designs and module specifications which describes the software that the purchaser hands over to the supplier.
- A whole subsystem into which another subsystem is to be integrated.
- A system which is to communicate with the system that is being developed.

Since the purchaser is supplying software, the supplier usually has a better chance of getting problems with that software rectified than if the software was supplied by some third party such as the vendor of a spreadsheet system. The quality system should reflect this fact.

8.2 PRE-CHECKING

The software supplier should aim to check any purchaser supplied software together with its documentation. This check would normally be carried out at the front end of the project, ideally as part of the bidding process for the project. It may be very difficult to check out the software at this stage but, certainly, the software supplier should aim to ask the purchaser for its documentation. The check would involve staff examining the documentation and assessing its quality in terms of readability and comprehensiveness. If the software documentation is poor, then there is a good chance that the purchaser supplied software will not be of the highest quality. If the supplier discovered that the documentation was of a poor quality then this would be an input into the planning process—particularly if the supplied software was a major component of the system to be developed. There are a number of implications for this in project planning.

First, the standards and procedures for planning should direct the project manager to consider the quality of the purchaser supplied documentation as an input to the process of taking actions after a risk analysis has been carried out; for example, by increasing the bid amount of the project and allocating extra time for staff who develop software that is to interface with the purchaser supplied product.

Second, the procedures for planning should result in those staff concerned with drawing up the contract for the developed system writing clauses into the contract to cater for possible poor functional performance of the supplied software. For example, a clause might be inserted in the contract which informed the purchaser that the supplier is not responsible for deficiencies in the supplied product, and that delays past a specified time due to problems being rectified in the supplied software would be accounted for and the purchaser invoiced.

Tips and techniques 14

It is a useful practice to include in the project plan a set of assumptions that the supplier is making about the behaviour of the purchaser together with a statement that if these assumptions are invalidated then the supplier cannot guarantee the specified delivery date. Some examples are: that any purchaser supplied product is correct; and that the purchaser will return documents which have been sent for approval within a certain time and will not cancel meetings.

Third, in the case where the software is a critical item and the supplier has discovered possible major problems during pre-checking, the supplier may insist on a formal system test before the purchaser supplied product is handed over, with the cost of the tests being billed to the purchaser.

Fourth, in the case where a purchaser supplies software which has no documentation, the procedures for planning should instruct the supplier to allow resources to be devoted to the development of this documentation.

8.3 PRODUCT IDENTIFICATION

All the components of a system should be identified properly. This is the subject of the next chapter. One part of this identification should be the source of the component. For example, it is common to insist as part of a programming standard that the originator of the software is identified in the comments attached to the program code. Both purchaser supplied source code and documentation should be identified as originating from the purchaser. It is also a good idea to have a file-naming convention that indicates whether documentation or program code stored in a particular file originated from the supplier, the purchaser or from some third party.

8.4 TESTING

Before purchaser supplied product is used with, or in, a developed system it should be tested. The level of testing that the software receives will depend on the documentation provided and the use which the supplier is to make of the software. For example, the purchaser may have provided a number of pre-written modules and the individual specifications for these modules. In this case the supplier carries out unit testing. However, if the purchaser supplies a whole subsystem together with a functional specification of that subsystem, then testing akin to system and acceptance testing would be carried out.

> **Tips and techniques 15**
>
> If you are really confident that some purchaser supplied product is of a very high quality, then some form of quick testing would be in order. One form of testing which does not require very much resource is known as *random testing*. With this form of testing the supplier uses data produced by software which generates random numbers, characters and strings. If the software does not crash and a small subset of the outputs from the random testing examined by the supplier are correct, then it is safe to assume that the software is of a high quality. However, it is worth warning you that this technique should only be used if you have a high confidence in the quality of the purchaser supplied software.

8.5 RELATION TO ISO 9000-3

ISO 9000-3 does not have very much to say about this part of the standard. One important point that it makes, however, is about the maintenance of the purchaser supplied product:

> Consideration should be given to the support of such software product in any maintenance agreement related to the product to be delivered.

This means that during the maintenance of the supplier-developed system there may be new versions of the purchaser supplied software being generated and that these should only be incorporated in any new versions of the system after thorough checking.

8.6 PROBLEMS

The problems which are encountered if this part of the standard is not adhered to are:

- Inadequately documented product is used in a system, leading to extra resource being spent during development detecting errors, delays to the project while the errors are rectified by either the supplier or the purchaser and an error-prone system being produced.
- Error-prone software is integrated into a developed system resulting in an overall error-prone system.
- Staff expend extra resources in determining the source of inadequately identified software.

8.7 CHECKS

- Standards and procedures exist for the pre-validation and checking of any product supplied by the purchaser—both software and its documentation.
- Guidelines exist which advise the project manager what to do when poor documentation and software is supplied by the purchaser.
- The risk analysis procedure includes actions to be taken if poor software or documentation is delivered by the purchaser.
- Guidelines for project planning describe the options which can be exercised if a software project has to cope with poorly specified or error-prone software.
- Guidelines exist which direct the project manager and legal staff on the measures to be taken in drawing up a contract for a system for which poorly specified or error-prone purchaser supplied software is to be included.
- Guidelines exist which advise the project manager what actions need to be taken during bidding, for a project which will include either poorly-specified or error-prone purchaser supplied software.
- Guidelines exist which provide advice on the level of testing to apply to purchaser supplied software and that standards and procedures are available which guide the process of testing.

9

PRODUCT IDENTIFICATION AND TRACEABILITY

9.1 INTRODUCTION

This part of the ISO 9001 standard deals with the way that documents on a software project are identified and how they are linked together. This part not only includes documents such as requirements specifications, system designs and acceptance test specifications, but also covers program code:

> Where appropriate the supplier shall establish and maintain procedures for identifying the product from applicable drawings, specifications or other documents, during all stages of production, delivery and installation.

9.2 PRODUCT IDENTIFICATION

> Where, and to the extent that, traceability is a specified requirement, individual product or batches shall have a unique identification. This identification shall be recorded.

All the configuration items in a system should have an identifier. Normally this identifier will have a number of components. The first component should be the name of the system which the item is associated with. The second would be some sort of designation which describes what form of document it is; for example, a design of a subsystem might have the designation *DES*. The next component would be the name of the configuration item. Thus the design of a subsystem which dealt with updating the stock in a warehouse might be called *DES StockUpdate*.

Next, each configuration item will have some form of version numbering. A simple scheme would give a configuration item the version number 1 when it was created, and increment the version number after an amendment or series of amendments have been applied. A more complicated version-numbering scheme would be the use of two numbers:

the first being a major version number with the second being a minor version number. For small changes the latter would be incremented by one, while for large changes the former would be incremented by one with the minor version number being reset to zero.

Another component of product identification would be some form of identification which showed that an item currently satisfied its requirements: that if the item was a program module, then it had been tested to ensure that it met its specification; or if the item was a subsystem design then that it had been reviewed to ensure that it met the relevant functional and non-functional requirements. Normally this form of identification would be implemented by single characters; for example, a C might indicate that an item conformed to its requirements and an N might indicate that the item had not yet been validated and currently did not conform to requirements.

These, then, are the main components of item identification. Normally the components of an identifier are linked by means of some separator such as a –. Thus, the module *Update* which forms part of the subsystem *StoresControl* that, in turn, forms part of the system *ProjectController*, which has been validated by means of testing and which exists in a version 1.3, would be identified as:

ProjectController – StoresControl – MODULE – Update – 1.3C

Such documentation rules are the major components which make up the identification of a configuration item. However, other information is often included, such as the name of the author of the item, the date the item was validated and a list of versions of the item. Normally documents have their identification placed prominently on their first page, with subsequent pages incorporating the identification, either in the headers or footers to the document. The identification of configuration items which are program code are written as comments—usually on the first page of the code; if sufficient documentation tools are available, then this information is also repeated in the headers or footers in the listing.

9.3 TRACEABILITY

One of the distinguishing features of a sophisticated quality system is that it maintains traceability between the documents and the program code which comprise a system under development. Before looking at how this is achieved it is worth describing the meaning of the term.

There are two forms of traceability. The first I shall call *document traceability*. This is where documents are identified in such a way that it is immediately obvious what the role of the document is in a system. For example, a good quality system should insist on standards which enable a member of the development staff to pick up a document and identify it, say, as a module in a particular subsystem x which makes up an overall system y. The previous section described a particular document identification convention which ensures that document traceability is present in the code or documentation produced for a system.

Document traceability is the easiest form of traceability to implement as it requires a relatively simple set of standards. The other form of traceability—functional traceability—is a little more difficult to built into a quality system. With *functional traceability* you can trace the functions that are in a requirements specification to the various parts of a system's documentation and to the program code of the system. An example will make this clear.

One of the things which I am asked to do as a consultant is to evaluate the quality system used by a software developer. Often this assessment provides information which may be used to determine whether the software developer is to be used as a subcontractor on a particular software project. There are two key questions that I ask which usually tells me whether a developer has a respectable quality system.

The first question is 'If I put my finger on a particular function which is described in your requirements specification can you tell me which modules in the completed system implement that function?' The second question is 'If I put my finger on a module in one of your completed systems can you tell me which functions in the requirements specification that module helps implement?' The first question explores something known as *forward functional traceability*, the ability to trace from a function into a later document or program code of a system; while the second question concerns something known as *reverse functional traceability*, the ability to trace backwards through a system's documentation, either from documents produced at the latest stage in the project or from program code.

Forward functional traceability is somewhat easier to implement than reverse functional traceability. However, they are both very important. It is worth looking at an example of how important they are. Assume that a project is reaching its later stages and staff are mainly involved in carrying out acceptance testing. Assume that during this process an error is discovered and programming staff modify a module in order that the error is rectified. The affected acceptance test—let us call it test n—is executed and the system passes the test. The unsophisticated developer would then be tempted to proceed with test $n + 1$. Unfortunately, this is not the correct thing to do since, in modifying the module, the programmer may inadvertently have inserted an error which, although it was not picked up by acceptance test n, affected a function or a series of functions which were tested by acceptance tests which preceded test n.

In order to determine which tests that precede test n need to be repeated, the developer needs to know which functions the module that was altered helps implement; this can only be achieved if the system documentation supports reverse functional traceability. If it does, the developer can pinpoint the functions involved and then, assuming that forward functional traceability is implemented, easily identify the names of the tests which check out these functions.

Forward and reverse traceability occur in a number of places in the documentation of a software project. You have already seen one example where the traceability between program code and functions was described. However, it also exists in testing documentation; for example, the traceability between a function, the system test that is used to test out the function, the test instructions for the test and the actual test data used for the test. There should be forward functional traceability all the way from the function down to the actual test data stored in some file.

Modern software development methods such as Yourdon Structured Development supports forward and reverse functional traceability. If you do not use such development methods, then you should not give up hope as there are a number of documentation techniques which can support both backward and forward traceability at little cost to the developer.

One means of documenting traceability is the verification matrix which was described on page 44. It consists of a tabular cross-listing of functions and modules which can be easily consulted to discover what modules a particular function uses. Normally the verification matrix is developed by a system designer after he or she has developed a design which implements the functions in a requirements specification. It thus offers more than just a facility for establishing traceability: it provides validation that a design meets the functional requirements of a system. A good project manager can breathe a sigh of relief when he or she hears that a good designer has completed the construction of a verification matrix.

Another way of establishing a limited form of forward and reverse functional traceability is to have standard naming conventions in the documentation that projects generate. For example, if functions are identified by means of a capital letter F followed by a number, then the outline test descriptions can be identified by preceding the function identifier by OT and the detailed tests associated with a particular outline test can be identified by the character D followed by the test number. The test data for a test would be stored in a file whose name is formed from the test name and the extension *tda*. Thus, OTF3D44.tda would be the name of the file which contains the test data for the 44th test which checks the function F3 in the requirements specification. This is just one example of a naming convention; many others exist. However, what is important is that the quality standards insist on a logical convention which *all* projects have to adhere to.

Tips and techniques 16

If you store your documents on computer files and specify that all document identities are enclosed within characters which are not normally used within these documents, such as double asterisks, then it is quite easy to develop a software tool which, given a particular item identification, will recover all the relevant documents that are related to that item. For example, if you are going to change a function in a requirements specification, then documents such as system test descriptions and test procedures for that function can be extracted automatically. This requires two pre-conditions: good document identification conventions such as those described in this section and a tool such as a programmable editor being readily available.

A developer who uses a verification matrix, or some variant, together with naming conventions which link entities such as functions, modules, tests, test data, test outcomes and test reports, has a quality system which addresses the concerns of this part of the ISO 9001 standard.

9.4 CONFIGURATION MANAGEMENT

While it is not explicitly stated in this part of the standard it is worth stating that identification of items should be based on the configuration items identified during the process of developing a configuration management plan. It is also worth restressing the fact that all items of documentation must come under configuration control, not just program code. This is one of the most common mistakes made by companies who submit themselves for ISO 9001 certification.

9.5 RELATION TO ISO 9000-3

The part of ISO 9000-3 which is relevant to this part of the standard is Section 6.1. This describes the process of configuration management. The component of configuration management which is known as configuration item identification is described in Section 6.1.1. This states that:

> The configuration management system should
>
> a) Identify uniquely the versions of each software item;
>
> b) Identify the versions of each software item which together constitute a specific version of a complete product;
>
> c) Identify the build status of software products in development or delivered and installed.

The term *software item* is normally used to describe any item which is placed under configuration control, for example a subsystem design or the program code of a module.

9.6 PROBLEMS

The problems which are encountered if this part of the standard is not adhered to are:

- Time is wasted in retrieving documents which have inadequate identification.
- Documents are used for developmental activities which have not yet been validated and are, hence, non-conforming. This would give rise to other documents or program code which are in error.
- Code is included in a delivered system which is non-conforming.
- Errors are not removed from a system after modification to program code, or a document such as a system design, has taken place.
- Extra effort is incurred by maintenance staff when functional enhancements are added to a system.
- Errors are committed by maintenance staff when functional enhancements are added to a system.

9.7 CHECKS

- Standards insist that every document and item of program code is properly identified.
- Version numbering, project identification and item identification information is included in each configuration item.
- Standards exist which make it relatively easy to trace from a function to the code which implements the function.
- Standards exist which make it relatively easy to trace from a module to the functions which the module helps implement.

- Standards exist which make it relatively easy to trace from a function to the test documentation for that function.
- Standards exist which make it relatively easy to trace from testing documentation to the functions that are tested.
- A procedure exists which insists that the developer places documentation under configuration control as well as program code.

10

PROCESS CONTROL

10.1 INTRODUCTION

This part of the standard directs the supplier to identify the individual processes that make up a software project, document them and specify standards for any documents or program code that are produced by a process. This section of the standard also deals with the detailed work instructions which are given to staff who are carrying out a particular process:

> The supplier shall identify and plan the production and, where applicable, installation processes which directly affect quality and shall ensure that these processes are carried out under controlled conditions.

The final part of this section of the standard also deals with special processes. These are processes whose results cannot be verified during a software project, but whose deficiencies can be identified during operation.

10.2 PROCESS IDENTIFICATION

I shall define a *process* as a software task which cannot be split further into atomic tasks. Thus, the design of a subsystem is not a process, since it can be split into a series of tasks concerned with the design of individual modules in a system. Since the design of the individual modules cannot be split further these can, hence, be regarded as processes. There are a wide variety of processes on a software project; examples include the design of a module, the programming of a module, the testing of a module, the review of a subsystem design and the production of a user manual.

A good quality system should contain procedures which direct the project manager to identify the individual processes that make up a software project. This identification should occur early in the software project—normally during the planning stage. Each process should be given an identifier, the amount of effort required to carry out a process estimated, the duration of the process specified and planning information such as the earliest start date, latest start date, earliest finish date and latest finish date.

As well as specifying information common to each task, development staff should also specify the relationship between each process and other processes that make up the software project. For example, whether a process follows another one, whether one process requires the completion of another process before it can be started and whether any process can be carried out in parallel with other processes. Once all this information has been specified it can be incorporated into some graphical medium such as a PERT network.

Tips and techniques 17

It is always worthwhile using PERT tools. There are a number of reasons for this: first, they impose a standard for process identification. If any member of staff violates this standard then the tool will produce an error message. Second, they allow for easy replanning. A large number of quality systems assume that planning only takes place at the beginning of a project. This is a myth. Replanning almost invariably takes place because of external circumstances such as a subcontractor delivering software late. Without a tool replanning can be very painful and is often avoided.

There are a number of tools which can process PERT networks and provide information such as whether a project is feasible in terms of timing and resources, whether certain staff are being allocated too much work on a day-by-day basis and the nature of the critical path of the project. The *critical path* is a series of processes which are carried out in sequence such that if there is any delay in one of the processes, the whole of the project is delayed. This is particularly useful information for the project manager, because he or she can then monitor the processes on the critical path more closely than other, less important processes. An extract from a procedure which describes the monitoring of important processes:

3.2 Critical processes

Some of the processes which will make up a software project will be critical in the sense that if they are delayed they will have an effect on the project in terms of delivery time and/or cost. These critical processes are normally identified in two ways. First, a project manager may have identified them as part of the risk analysis procedure used in planning (see Section 2.3.1) or they may have been identified by the ProjectPlan tool as being on a critical path. Whatever the source of identification it is worth paying special attention to these processes during the execution of a project.

This special attention may take a number of forms. First, these processes will need to be monitored more frequently. It is often worthwhile calling for reports on these processes at a more frequent rate than might be normal. Second, it is worth assigning your best staff to a process. Third, there will be some processes under less control of the manager, for example a process carried out by a subcontractor. In this case it is worth employing some of the risk reduction techniques outlined in Section 2.3.2 of this manual, for example ensuring that the contract with a subcontractor contains clauses which give rise to financial penalties which can be used to employ internal staff in order to enable a project to catch up.

Another issue concerned with software processes is that each process should be described by work instructions which are given to the staff who are to carry out the process. For example, a member of the developmental staff who is to carry out the task of module programming should be provided with instructions which detail: where the module specification that is to be programmed can be found; where in the project library to deposit test data and test files; whether any special tests are needed; and what to do if the module specification which has been provided is deficient in some way. Much of this information can be found in the quality plan of the project. However, some of the information, for example any special instructions for testing, is normally included in detailed working instructions that are provided to staff carrying out a process.

This part of the standard is also concerned with the monitoring and control of processes; that is, ensuring that standards and procedures are in place which enable the project manager to monitor the progress of a project. During project planning the project manager will have identified the individual processes which make up a project. During the execution of a project staff will be completing processes and a good quality system should insist that once a process has been completed the staff who were involved in that process fill in some documentation which provides primitive information that can then be used to monitor the progress of the project. For example, useful information would be the day that work was started on a process, the day that work was completed and the amount of time spent on the process. This documentation can then be collected and used to track project progress against planning information. It can be used by the project manager to determine an estimated completion date, a projected amount of resources that will be used by the project, the amount of resources used up so far and any slippage of time and resource.

10.3 STANDARDS FOR PROCESS PRODUCTS

This part of the standard states that each type of process which is to be carried out and which produces some product—such as a coded module or a test suite—should be associated with a standard for the product which is to be developed. Standards should exist for at least the following items:

- *The requirements specification.* It should insist on a formal layout for the part of this document which describes the functions of the system. This is normally expressed as a functional hierarchy in which main functions are split into subfunctions which are, in turn, split into sub-subfunctions, and so on. This standard should also specify all the other possible sections in the requirements specification for non-functional requirements such as response time, memory occupancy, file occupancy, reliability, and so on. A final part of the standard for the requirements specification should describe the way in which data is to be described. For example, the requirements specification standard should show how two data entities are related to each other. A good example of this is in an air-traffic control system where each air-traffic controller is associated with n flights which are either incoming or outgoing: the requirements specification should specify this relation.

- *The system design.* The standard for the system design should describe the modules that will be in the system, what each module does and the relationship between the modules. For example, for a third-generation programming language the modules will be subroutines and the description of each subroutine will describe the function of each module, the parameters of each subroutine, the subroutines which each subroutine calls, the subroutines which call the subroutine and a description of the interface between subroutines and global variables.

  For a fourth-generation language the system design will consist of descriptions of each of the programs which are to be coded together with their associated data. This data is normally specified as tables when the target language is a fourth-generation language.

- *The test documentation.* The standards should describe what should be included in the test documentation for system tests, acceptance tests and module tests. This is described in more detail in Chapter 17.

- *Programming standards for each of the programming languages which are used by the software supplier.* These should specify the layout of lines of program code, variable naming conventions, the comments that should be included in a module, the indentation to be used for laying out control structures and the provision of information about such things as the identities of global variables that are manipulated by a subroutine.

Tips and techniques 18

Many large word processors contain an outliner facility. This enables the user of the word processor to build up a document hierarchically. The user first specifies the text at the top level of the hierarchy, then fills in the text at the next level and so on. The levels are then displayed numerically, with top levels being associated with a single digit and the next level associated with two digits, and so on. For example, a function for monitoring temperatures in a chemical process system might be given the level number 3 with all the subfunctions of this function being numbered 3.1, 3.2, etc. An outliner enables levels to be moved, text to be inserted at a level, text to be deleted from a level and the hierarchy displayed with different levels having different layout styles. This leads to extremely readable documentation. A large amount of documentation on a software project can be expressed hierarchically, not just the functional specification, and it is always worthwhile using an outliner to organize it.

10.4 SPECIAL PROCESSES

A part of this section of the ISO 9001 standard describes processes which are known as special processes. These are processes whose results cannot be validated during a project, but whose effectiveness can only be judged when the software system is in use. These processes are found very infrequently on software projects. One example of this occurs where a software purchaser specifies that a system should have a particular mean-time between serious failure which is, say, 2 years. If the software project that produces a system of this criticality only lasts six months, then there will be a problem with satisfying this requirement. Although there are some mathematical theories which have been developed which are able to give approximate values for reliability, they are sufficiently novel that they cannot be relied upon.

Another example of a special process occurs when a purchaser wants a system which is to be run on special hardware that has not yet been released by its manufacturer, and is due to be released after the project is targeted to finish, but where a similar hardware configuration is readily available from the purchaser. If the purchaser wanted a certain response time from the future hardware, then the only checks that could be carried out are those on the existing hardware and some form of extrapolation could be used.

This form of response-time testing is a special process because the software supplier does not have 100% confidence that the future hardware will achieve the desired response time. The implication from this part of the standard is that special processes should be identified, documented in the project plan and the purchaser warned about their nature. Provision should also be made in the contract for extra work to be carried out by the supplier in the event of tasks carried out as a special process not providing the correct results. For example, in the example of hardware that has not yet been released, the contract between the supplier and the purchaser should specify that in the event of the performance of the system on the new hardware not being of the level specified in the requirements specification then the supplier will provide resource to tune the software so that it does meet performance requirements, and that this resource will be paid for jointly by the purchaser and the supplier.

10.5 RELATION TO ISO 9000-3

There are three sections of ISO 9000-3 which are relevant to this part of the standard. They are Sections 5.6, 6.5 and 6.6. Section 5.6 stresses that adequate standards are used for design and implementation and that the development method used should suit the application area. An important section is 5.6.4 which promotes reviews:

> The supplier should carry out reviews to ensure that the requirements are met and the above methods are correctly carried out. The design or implementation process should not proceed until the consequences of all known deficiencies are satisfactorily resolved or the risk of proceeding otherwise known.

Section 6.5 is merely a statement which, in effect, states that the software developer should use adequate standards and procedures. It also makes a plea for the revision of this part of the quality system:

> The supplier should provide rules, practices and conventions in order to make the quality system specified in this part of ISO 9000 effective. The supplier should review these rules, practices and conventions and revise them as required.

Section 6.6 advocates the use of tools for making the quality system effective. No tools are specified, but the implication here is that tools such as PERT packages, CASE tools and testing tools have a place within the development and management of a software project.

10.6 PROBLEMS

The problems which are encountered if this part of the standard is not adhered to are:

- Without adequate standards and procedures for process identification and documentation the project manager has major problems in costing a project.
- Without adequate standards and procedures for process identification and documentation the project manager has major problems in monitoring the progress of a project in terms of time and resources.
- Without an adequate means of documenting the relationship between processes the project manager will find major problems if he or she has to replan a project.
- Without an adequate means of documenting processes the project manager has major problems in determining the feasibility of a project in terms of resources available and resources required.
- Without adequate work instructions staff carry out substandard work leading to errors in the tasks they have currently been assigned to.
- Without adequate standards which, for example, define the form of a particular document such as a system design, staff assigned to tasks such as requirements specification expend unnecessary resources and commit errors which would not have occurred with better standards.
- Without a procedure for identifying special processes there is the danger that the software company will sign a contract which contains requirements that they are unable to guarantee can be met. If a procedure for identifying special processes exists, then the software supplier has less chance of being involved in litigation when the product of a special process is unable to meet requirements.

10.7 CHECKS

- Standards and procedures exist which describe how processes in a software project are identified and documented. These standards and procedures are usually contained in that part of the quality manual concerned with planning.
- Standards and procedures exist for the reporting of completion of a particular process and the amount of resources expended.
- Standards exist for the description of work instructions for each type of process in a software project.
- Standards exist which define the layout of major items in the software project, such as the system design and the code of modules.
- A procedure exists which enables a project manager to identify special processes during planning, and ensures that the software supplier does not commit himself or herself to a delivered system whose properties depend on special processes.

11

INSPECTION AND TESTING

11.1 INTRODUCTION

This section of the ISO 9000 standard concerns the validation of the software product. A narrow interpretation of the standard for software development would confine its attention to testing. However, it is much more useful to interpret it as including all validation activities, of which testing will be the main component. There are four testing activities which the standard covers: system testing, acceptance testing, unit testing and integration testing; it also covers the conduct of technical reviews, inspections or walkthroughs.

11.2 RECEIVING INSPECTION AND TESTING

A software supplier will often receive system components from other sources. These sources will include the purchaser, software supplied by commercial package suppliers, subcontractors, public domain software suppliers and software libraries. It is important that any software received into a project is thoroughly tested before it is incorporated into a system:

> The supplier shall ensure that incoming product is not used or processed (except in the circumstances described in 4.10.1.2) until it has been inspected or otherwise verified as conforming to specified requirements.

The reason for this is clear: if the incorporated software is of a lesser quality than that developed for the system, then it will become a weak link and be the source of major defects.

The supplier should have standards and procedures in place which determine the level of testing required for a software product and describe the process of testing software received from external sources. The level of testing will depend on the source of the software and the criticality of the system that is to be developed. For example, if the project develops safety-critical software, then all received software should be thoroughly tested, including software from reputable manufacturers and software from highly-validated libraries. However, if the software was for a less critical system, or formed the non-safety critical part of a safety-critical system and was developed by a software subcontractor who had a very high reputation, then the testing of that software would obviously be less rigorous.

The quality system should provide directions to the software project staff to examine the nature of all received software and should provide standards and procedures which govern the derivation of what is, effectively, an acceptance test suite for that software. The quality system should also describe what actions should be carried out if any received software was found defective.

The tests that are carried out on incoming software should be documented in the quality plan for a project.

11.3 IN-PROCESS INSPECTION AND TESTING

This part of the ISO 9000 standard is relevant to developmental testing: the testing that takes place during the programming stage of the software project which checks that particular developmental tasks have been carried out adequately. The two test activities which this part of the standard addresses are unit testing and integration testing. The standard states that the supplier shall:

> inspect, test and identify product as required by the quality plan or documented procedures

and

> establish product conformance to specified requirements by use of process monitoring and control methods.

Standards and procedures should exist which specify how these tasks are to be carried out and what documentation is to emerge that demonstrates that they have been carried out correctly. For example, the quality system should provide guidance on the integration strategy that is to be adopted: i.e. what criteria determine whether a system is to be integrated from the top-level modules downwards or from the bottom-level modules upwards; what documentation is generated to show the progression of the integration; and how the various integration tests which check out the interfaces between modules are to be documented.

An example of the sort of level of detail which is found in a testing procedure is shown here. It is a fragment from a procedure which describes integration testing:

5.4 Integration procedure

5.4.1 Integration
Unless there is a very good reason for not doing it, all our projects should integrate subroutines

which have been produced by programmers. If a project manager decides not to integrate he or she should contact his or her technical manager and give good reason before deciding on this course of action.

Integration is planned after the overall system design has been frozen and comes under configuration control. There are a number of decisions that a project manager or designer has to make regarding integration:

1. What form of integration to adopt. There are essentially three strategies which we use. The pros and cons of each strategy are detailed below in Sections 5.4.2 to 5.4.4.
2. The order in which integration is to occur. Given that a project manager has chosen the strategy there is still considerable leeway as to the order in which subroutines are inserted.
3. The number of subroutines which are to be added at a time.

A number of inputs have to be considered before addressing the last two points. First, it is necessary to determine the information needed which drives a consideration of the number of modules to be integrated at a time. Normally, an integration strategy should not involve the integration of more than 10 modules at a time. Integrations over that limit often mean that errors in some of the subroutines that are integrated may interact with each other to produce subtle effects that reduce the effectiveness of debugging.

There are two ways of carrying out integration. The first is to assume that each integration will always involve n modules. The value of n will be determined by the overall complexity of the subroutines in the system. For a system with a large number of modules with complex processing code and big interfaces n will be low. For a system consisting, in the main, of single-function subroutines n will tend towards a high level.

The second option which can be adopted is to specify that the normal number of modules that will be integrated will usually be n, but that very complex modules, identified by the designer, will be integrated singly or with a small number of other modules. This strategy is suitable for a system with a large number of not very complex subroutines, but with a few large ones.

The second point, the order in which the subroutines are integrated, may be constrained by programmer availability: for example, you may know that some subroutines will be produced by a programmer who is joining the project late. However, if planning is carried out well there should be quite a degree of leeway for the order of integration.

In considering the order of integration the designer or project manager should bear in mind two criteria: the criticality of the functions that are contained in the system and the importance of the functions. For example, we normally integrate our systems in a top-down fashion. Also, the systems we produce tend to have the human–computer interface embedded in the top-level modules. If there is a feeling that the customer has not quite correctly communicated some of the functions, then the top-level modules which implement the interface for these functions should be integrated first.

The second criterion is that of importance of functions. As part of the project planning procedure the project manager will have carried out a risk analysis of the project (see Project Procedures Section 13.3). If the project is a high-risk project, then a good strategy to adopt is to integrate the system in such a way that the important functions of the system are integrated first, followed by the next important functions, and so on. In this way if the project starts looking as if it is heading for trouble in terms of lateness, the project manager can ask the customer whether he or she wishes to have a delivery of the software that has so far been integrated, after some acceptance testing has, of course, taken place.

As part of the analysis (see Analysis Procedures Section 11.1), analysts for a high-risk project will have ordered the system functions in decreasing order of importance; these details can be found in Section 7.3 of the requirements specification.

5.4.2 Top-down integration

There are a large number of reasons for adopting top-down integration:

1. The system does not require any extra software to hold it together. The system is, in effect, its own test bed. In the past, with bottom-up integration, we have found that we have had to produce scaffold software which has been as large as 40% of the final system size.

2. It enables us to demonstrate the human–computer interface to the customer at a relatively early stage of the project. The vast majority of our systems have this interface embedded in top-level modules.

3. You have a working version of the system from the moment that the first integration has been correctly tested.

4. It provides an extra fillip to a project. If a project is particularly lengthy you will find staff morale dropping somewhere during the middle of the project because of the perceived lack of progress in terms of executable code. The news that the first version of the system—albeit the first few modules which form the initial integration—is working has a surprising effect on staff morale.

5. It is able to detect top-level control and sequencing errors better than the other forms of integration that our quality manual describes.

Tips and techniques 19

It is always worthwhile storing all the test data generated by a project on some file medium. It takes only a little effort, especially if you use playback tools. However, it can save weeks if not months of time when project changes or requirements changes necessitate modification to a system.

For unit testing the quality manual should contain guidelines on: the testing techniques to be used; the way that tests are to be documented; and how the test data, test outcomes and any test harnesses are to be stored in the project library in case any retesting needs to take place.

11.4 FINAL INSPECTION AND TESTING

The implication of this section is that the software supplier should establish the properties of the system that need to be tested, plan for the execution of the system and acceptance tests and carry out the tests at the end of the software project:

> The supplier shall carry out all final inspection and testing in accordance with the quality plan or documented procedures to complete the evidence of conformance of the finished product to the specified requirements.

The final testing process is split into two activities: system testing and acceptance testing. The former is a test of those properties of the system which are expressed in the requirements specification within the supplier's premises; the latter are a test of the properties of the system within the environment in which the system is to be embedded. Normally the acceptance tests are witnessed by the purchaser.

Standards and procedures should be in place which direct the supplier to extract the requirements to be tested from the requirements specification and express them in such a form that they can be expanded out to detailed test instructions. Normally the requirements to be tested are extracted from the requirements specification at an early stage, and are gradually transformed into test instructions and test data files during the software project. The quality system should specify standards for the documents which are to hold this information and also describe procedures which detail the transformation from high-level requirements into test instructions—including what actions are to be taken if the staff charged with developing the test instructions have problems in extracting them from the requirements specification.

11.5 INSPECTION AND TEST RECORDS

It is important that all testing activities give rise to documentation which demonstrates that the tests have taken place and have been carried out correctly. This directive is not only important for system and acceptance testing, but is important for developmental testing activities such as unit testing. It is worth examining the test records for each of these activities in order:

> The supplier shall establish and maintain records which give evidence that the product has passed inspection and/or test with defined acceptance criteria.

For example, it should be possible for someone to look at the records of a software project and, for each module, discover whether any unit testing took place and whether that testing was adequate. There should be enough documentation available which can help a project manager or a member of the quality staff discern whether a module was tested thoroughly and not just clean-compiled and handed over to the staff involved in system testing.

There are a number of ways of ensuring this. Normally, the documentation for the module should include: a clean compiled version of the module; a description of the test data produced by the programmer who produced the module; and the location of the test data file and the file containing the test outcomes. This information can be examined by staff who have to sign-off the module as being adequately developed and tested.

Tips and techniques 20

One way of documenting that a unit test has been carried out is to employ a dynamic analyser. This is a tool that instruments the code of software that is to be tested and produces reports which describe the structural coverage that has been achieved by the test. Normally this is in the form of a histogram which shows the frequency of execution of each statement or branch in a program. The output from such a tool can be stored easily and provides evidence that thorough testing has taken place.

Similar documentation can be used for the test records generated by system and acceptance testing. The important point again is that someone can visit a project and discern quickly that a particular test has taken place and that it has been successfully completed. For system and acceptance testing this means that the quality system should provide standards for test reporting. For example, the quality system should insist on problem report forms being issued when a test fails and a test log filled in for each test

Update command name ok	✓	✓	✓	×
Parameter 1 ok	✓	×		
Parameter 2 ok	✓		×	
Command error				✓
Parameter error		✓	✓	
Update executed	✓			

Table 11.1 A decision table

that was carried out. The quality system should also insist that test data should be stored in the project library together with any test outcomes. The existence of this documentation together with the existence of the test files is usually enough evidence that a test has taken place and was competently carried out.

Tips and techniques 21

A convenient way of documenting the functional tests for a system is by using a table known as a *decision table*. Such a table consists of conditions and actions separated by a double line. Each column in the table describes what action is to be taken if a series of conditions holds. For example, Table 11.1 documents the tests for a command which has two parameters and which, if the command name is typed in correctly and the parameters are valid, will update a database. Each column describes a particular event that can occur with this function. A tick stands for the fact that a particular statement is true, while a cross stands for the fact that a statement is false. For example, in the second column the decision table specifies that if the update command is typed in correctly but the first parameter provided by the user is incorrect, then a parameter error will occur. Normally decision tables are written for each function in a system and not for the whole system, since the resulting size of decision table would be prohibitive. There are a number of advantages to this form of documentation. First, it is easy to understand by both the supplier and the purchaser. Second, it can be automated by storing the table in a spreadsheet.

For integration testing there is a similar requirement: that test data is stored and that documentation is generated when a test is carried out successfully or when a test fails. However, the level of detail of this documentation will normally be lower than for other forms of testing since integration testing is usually the least important form of testing that occurs on the software project. Technical reviews should also generate records which demonstrate that validation has taken place. Normally these records would be the minutes of the review, together with a list of defects discovered during the review. The quality system should provide procedures and standards which ensure that there is documentation generated which confirms that any errors which were discovered were removed and validated. For example, a technical review may have discovered only a few errors.

Normally the chair of the review will not hold a re-review, but will check that the member of staff who committed the errors has rectified them. When this check is completed the review chair will sign off the modifications and attach them as an appendix to the review minutes. If the review discovered a large number of errors, then another review would be held and the minutes of that review would form the record that validation has taken place.

11.6 RELATION TO ISO 9000-3

The relevant sections of ISO 9000-3 are Sections 5.7, 5.8 and 5.9. Section 5.7 describes the fact that there are number of testing activities associated with a software project, but is not prescriptive in describing them. It places great stress on the fact that a software supplier has to carry out detailed planning for all testing activities. This includes the derivation of test cases, the description of the tests, the software and hardware environments used, test acceptance criteria and the staff resources required. It also specifies that the linked processes of error discovery, the transmission of error reports, modification and retesting should be paid special attention to. The final two subsections, 5.7.4 and 5.7.5, describe the fact that system testing should be carried out:

> Before offering the product for delivery and purchaser acceptance, the supplier should validate its operation as a complete product, when possible under conditions similar to the application environment as specified in the contract.

It also specifies that when field testing is carried out the features to be tested should be documented and the responsibilities of both the supplier and the purchaser with respect to this form of testing should also be documented—normally in the test plan.

Section 5.8 describes acceptance testing. It specifies that it should be carried out according to agreed test acceptance criteria and the process of mediating and acting on errors by the supplier and the purchaser be agreed beforehand. This is normally documented in the quality plan. This section also stresses the need for planning in terms of timing of testing tasks, procedures for acceptance and the hardware and software environment used. Again, this information would be placed in the test plan.

Finally, Subsection 5.9.2 places stress on final checking before delivery: that there should be some procedure which ensures that the correct modules and versions of modules are incorporated into the system which is to be delivered to the purchaser. This normally means that two checks are carried out: a visual check of the version numbers and identities of the modules included in the delivered software and also a few perfunctory tests of the functionality of the delivered software to ensure that no gross errors have been made in assembling the modules.

11.7 PROBLEMS

The problems which are encountered if this part of the standard is not adhered to are:

- Poor items of software from other sources are incorporated into a final system, with these items giving rise to major quality problems such as exhibiting errors in functionality.

- Inadequate direction is given to staff carrying out unit testing. This results in the production of modules which are in error.

- Poor quality records are produced from unit testing. This gives rise to problems in providing assurance that the system is of a high quality, and allows programming staff to be less thorough than they would be if good quality records were produced.

- Inadequate direction is given to staff carrying out integration testing. This results in errors being present in the interfaces between modules and between the system and the outside world.

- Poor quality records are produced from unit testing. This gives rise to problems in providing assurance that the system is of a high quality and allows staff charged with unit testing to be less thorough than they would be if good quality records were produced.

- Inadequate tests are generated for unit and integration testing. This leads to residual errors which will either be present in the final system, or will take much more resource to remove during system and acceptance testing.

- Inadequate system testing takes place, with the result that errors which should have been detected during this testing phase are detected in front of the purchaser during acceptance testing.

- Inadequate quality records are generated by technical reviews. The absence of such records will provide a lower level assurance of the quality of a system and lead to residual errors. Their absence also removes a potential source of data that can be used to evaluate the operation of a quality system.

- Poor quality records are produced from system and acceptance testing. This gives rise to problems in providing assurance that the system is of a high quality and allows staff charged with system and acceptance testing to be less thorough than they would be if good quality records were produced.

- System and acceptance tests do not reflect the functional and non-functional requirements specified in the requirements specification.

11.8 CHECKS

- Standards and procedures exist which detail how requirements in the requirements specification are extracted, documented and expanded out into system and acceptance tests.

- Standards and procedures exist which detail how system tests and acceptance tests are applied and the results of the test documented.

- Standards and procedures exist which detail how unit tests are applied and how the results of the tests are documented.

- Standards and procedures exist which detail how integration tests are applied and how the results of the tests are documented.

- Procedures exist which detail what should happen when a test fails.

- Standards and procedures exist which detail what a project manager should do when his or her software project contains software from other sources. These standards and procedures should cover the tests that have to be carried out in order to discern whether this software is of a comparable quality to that generated by the project.
- Standards and procedures exist which direct the project manager on the contents of the test plan and how to develop this plan.

12

INSPECTION, MEASURING AND TEST EQUIPMENT

12.1 INTRODUCTION

Of all the sections in the ISO 9001 standard this is the one which, at first sight, seems rather irrelevant to the development of software. It is concerned with the reliability of measuring equipment on a project:

> The supplier shall control, calibrate and maintain inspection, measuring and test equipment, whether owned by the supplier, on loan, or provided by the purchaser, to demonstrate the conformance of product to the specified requirements.

It conjures up images of instruments being sent to calibration laboratories, engineers measuring tolerances of machine tools and the use of engineering jigs. While this part of the standard is most relevant to the conventional engineering sector, it does contain some important messages for the software supplier. Before examining this relevance it is worth describing some of the testing tools that are available to the software supplier. Many of them are commercial products; however, many primitive examples of these tools can be developed by a software supplier—either for general, in-house use or for a specific project:

- *Dynamic analysers.* These are software tools which instrument a chunk of software and provide information about what structural elements of that software have been executed. For example, a dynamic analyser will tell you the percentage of statements that have been executed by a particular test data set. Many analysers will also provide a histogram which gives the number of executions of each structural element.
- *Static analysers.* These are tools which process source code and provide validation and quality control information without executing the source code. These tools range in sophistication from simple tools which provide quality metrics to sophisticated static analysers which detect errors such as non-initialized variables and the presence of program code which can never be executed.

- *Test harnesses.* These are software tools which take a chunk of code which cannot immediately be executed, for example a module, and enclose it with statements that make it executable. These test harnesses will also add statements that direct test data to the software under test and monitor the results from the tests.
- *Test librarians.* These are tools which store files of test data from integration, unit, system or acceptance testing and are normally associated with software tools which are capable of carrying out retests automatically.
- *Test data generators.* These are tools which generate large files of test data. They are normally used for system testing and are particularly useful for performance testing. The more sophisticated tools are capable of generating test data to a specified statistical pattern.
- *Simulators.* These tools simulate some piece of hardware or even another software system which provides data to be processed by the system under test. These tools are often developed within a software project, and are often used for performance testing.
- *Debugging tools.* These tools are usually specific to an operating system or a particular dialect of a programming language. They display values of variables, allow break points to be set and monitor the execution of a chunk of software. The majority are commercially produced, although I have occasionally found that software suppliers who make extensive use of a particular programming language implementation will have developed primitive debugging tools of their own.

In the standard and in this book a broad interpretation of the term *tool* is that it not only encompasses the categories of software described above, but also any piece of software which is used to support the testing process, for example a program which is used to examine a database after a particular test has been executed or some program statements which are written by the programmer to act as a test harness.

Tips and techniques 22

A technique which is particularly useful in a third-generation language environment is to use a word processor with a glossary facility to prepare programs and modules. A glossary is a pre-stored set of text which can be inserted into a document with little effort, usually by one or two key presses or mouse clicks. Templates for all sorts of documentation can be held as glossary items; for example, much of the enclosing software required to turn a module into a program ready for execution during unit testing can be placed in a glossary.

12.2 IDENTIFICATION OF TESTING TOOLS

The implication of this part of the standard is that during an early part of the project— normally project planning—the software supplier should identify the need for certain testing tools on a software project and should either plan for their acquisition or development. Normally planning for acquisition is simple: the supplier specifies a task which covers the ordering of the tool from its commercial suppliers.

For a testing tool which is to be developed by a project what is required is a plan for specifying, designing, implementing and testing the tool to be developed, using at least the same standards and procedures which are to be employed on the project which is to use the tool. This is particularly important for specifying what the tool should do. This plan may be part of the overall project plan, or may exist separately from it if, for example, the team charged with developing the tool is separate from the team that is developing the system which is to be tested. It is also important when planning a project that the cost of acquiring or developing a tool, and training staff in its use, is added to the overall cost of the project.

Many of the concerns of this section of the standard with commercial software tools are very relevant to those which deal with software product which is purchased.

12.3 DEVELOPING A TEST TOOL

This part of the ISO 9001 standard implies that the development of any test tools should be at least of the standard as that used on the project which uses the test tool. That is, similar standards for requirements specification, system design, programming and testing should be employed, and the same quality records generated. If the test tool is a critical element to a project in that it is used frequently, then a software supplier will often decide to impose heavier quality assurance than that employed on the main software project, particularly if the supplier has identified a need for the tool on a number of future projects.

12.4 VALIDATING A TESTING TOOL

If a testing tool is to be used to provide evidence that some property of the system to be developed has been satisfied, then it is important that some degree of confidence that the tool is itself correct should be required by the software supplier.

The degree of confidence depends on the use to which the tool is to be put, the criticality of the application and the source of the tool. For a tool which is developed by the supplier for a safety-critical system that checks the functional correctness of the software, the degree of validation will be very high and will, almost certainly, at least match the level applied to the software produced by the supplier. For a tool which enforces testing standards, that is to be used on a clerical application and bought-in from a reputable supplier who has sold hundreds of copies of the tool, the amount of validation would be very small—if not negligible. What would be required in this case would be an entry in the project quality plan which provided an explanation of why little or no validation is to take place.

Whatever the nature of the testing tools to be used on a software project, the planning procedures should instruct the project manager to provide a rationale which describes why the degree of validation chosen for the tool was decided upon. For high levels of validation the manager should be instructed to incorporate the quality controls in the overall project plan.

12.5 CONFIGURATION MANAGEMENT OF TESTING TOOLS

Testing tools developed by a supplier should be regarded as a configuration item and come under the same configuration control as other configuration items. This means that if changes occur to the tools, then these changes are rigorously controlled and the tool is tested to ensure that the changes only affect the areas of the tool for which they are intended.

For tools which have been bought in—particularly those for critical applications—there is a requirement on the software supplier to retest these tools each time a new version is delivered to the supplier. This can be done by running a small subset of past tests and checking that the output from the new version of the tool matches the old output.

12.6 RELATION TO ISO 9000-3

The sections which are relevant to this part of the standard are Sections 5.7 and 6.6. Section 5.7 is a general directive about the testing process but does, in Subsection 5.7.2, indicate that the supplier should plan for the use of software testing tools if they are to be employed on a project. For example, if they are to be developed by the supplier, then the tasks which make up the development should be identified and timetabled.

Section 6.6 is a general directive that the supplier should make appropriate use of tools in order to make the guidelines of ISO 9000-3 effective. All that this means is that the developer should examine the quality factors for a particular project and discover whether any quality controls require tool support.

12.7 PROBLEMS

The problems which are encountered if this part of the standard is not adhered to are:

- Software testing tools are developed by the supplier which are in error and which do not adequately support the testing process. At the very worst such tools may provide erroneous evidence that a test was successful.
- Inadequate specification of the properties of a testing tool is produced, resulting in the development or purchase of a tool which does not carry out its functions.
- Inadequate checking of a testing tool resulting in errors which affect the validation carried out by the supplier.
- Tools are purchased from inadequate sources which do not carry out their promised functions. This could either lead to project delays or to errors not being detected during testing.
- Changes to testing tools cause errors which delay a software project or result in the delivered product containing errors.

12.8 CHECKS

- The project planning standards and procedures specify that all internally developed testing tools are produced using at least the same degree of quality control as the project in which they are to be used.
- The planning procedures include a section on the specification of testing tools which are either bought in from outside suppliers or are developed internally. This section could be subsumed in a general section about the process of buying in or developing any software used for support.
- Guidelines exist which enable the project manager to decide whether a software testing tool is to be developed internally or purchased.
- The configuration management standards and procedures specify that any internally developed testing tools should be regarded as configuration items.

13

INSPECTION AND TEST STATUS

13.1 INTRODUCTION

This part of the standard is concerned with the identification of the status of software and documentation which is to be validated. It is important to point out that this part of the standard can also be interpreted to cover the status of the documentation which accompanies a system:

> The inspection and test status of product shall be identified by using markings, authorized stamps, tags, labels, routing cards, inspection records, test software, physical location or other suitable means, which indicate the conformance or nonconformance of product with regard to inspection and tests performed.

The ultimate test of whether a quality system satisfies this part of the standard is to ask how long it would normally take for someone unfamiliar with a project to discover the status of, say, a module. If it takes a few minutes to discover that the module was not yet coded, coded but not tested or fully tested, then the quality system would normally conform to ISO 9001 requirements.

13.2 TEST STATUS

Test items will normally be modules, subsystems, a whole subsystem and a build of a system. The term *build* describes part of a system which has been integrated. Many companies which make full use of integration will define a number of builds, each of which contains a number of modules that have been integrated and integration tested. Normally builds correspond to subsystems; however, some software developers will define a series of builds based on implementing a set of similar functions. For example, a software developer will define build n of a software system as build $n - 1$ together with modules which implement query functions.

The standards for programming, unit testing, integration testing, system testing and acceptance testing should insist that the test status of an item of software should be easily retrieved. For modules the programming standard should insist that a comment is inserted into the header of the module which gives its status. Normally, two values for this status would be acceptable: *programmed* and *tested*. All that would be needed to check on the status of a module would be to look at this comment.

Similar measures can be taken for indicating the test status of a build. There are two options for this: using a file-naming convention or keeping track of build test status by means of documentation. The first option involves having a file-naming convention for builds and augmenting the file names of files containing the source and object code of the build to indicate test status. For example, the quality system may insist that the file names of files containing builds will be of the form *bunnn.bux*, where *nnn* is a three-digit number that represents the number of the build, with x being u if the build has not been fully tested, i.e. if all the modules have not been added to the previous build and all the integration tests have not been carried out. x might be t if the build is complete and fully tested. Thus, *bu012.but* would represent build 12 of a system which had been fully tested.

An alternative to using a file-naming convention is to keep documentation which describes a build's status. This documentation would be simple: it would consist of a few sheets of paper which lists the builds and their test statuses. Other information could also be kept, such as the date when the build was regarded as fully tested. It is a matter of taste which convention is to be adopted. The only objection I have heard against the file-naming convention approach is that staff need to have immediate access to a central computer or file server to obtain the information and that paper documentation is easier to find. My own experience is the reverse. However, if you are confident that your staff have excellent filing systems the second solution may be the best.

For system and acceptance tests a documentation solution is usually the best solution. By the time system testing is ready to be started, the software developer will have constructed a set of tests which fully check out both the functional and non-functional properties of a system. These tests will be applied during the later stages of the project, with the success and failure of a test being determined by written documentation which describes what the result of a test should be. The test status of a system can easily be determined by ensuring that a summary sheet is kept up to date which contains the number of system tests to be carried out, the number of tests which have been successfully applied and the number of tests which have failed. From this, development staff and managerial staff are able to determine exactly what the test status of the system is with respect to system testing. If the system tests are applied only at the subsystem level, then each subsystem would be associated with a separate piece of documentation.

For acceptance testing a similar scheme can be adopted. Normally acceptance testing is carried out at the system level rather than the subsystem level, so that only one item of documentation would be needed.

13.3 INSPECTION STATUS

There will be a number of documents which are generated during the software project that require an inspection status. These include documents such as the requirements specification, system design, system test plan and configuration plan. Important documents such as these should receive a degree of validation determined by the quality plan.

Tips and techniques 23

A spreadsheet package is an excellent aid for maintaining quality documentation. For example, the documentation for keeping track of test and inspection status described in this chapter can be placed in a spreadsheet. Most modern spreadsheet packages have a primitive programming language attached to them and can be used to display important information. For example, a program for a spreadsheet language could easily be developed which displayed all the names of software items which have been programmed but not yet tested. A word of warning, however: do not be in too much of a hurry to computerize your quality system. It is quite a difficult task to implement or make major changes to a quality system, requiring technical, political and social skills, and adding to the burden by computerizing will increase the chances that the implementation or modification will not be totally successful. Get the quality system right first and then *gradually* computerize those parts which are amenable to automation.

It is important that standards exist which require project staff to document the status of all these documents. For simple items all that is necessary is for some part of the cover sheet to contain the signature of the person who has validated the document. For larger documents which are split into subdocuments, for example a system design split into subsystem designs, the subdocuments should have cover sheets for signing-off with information about which reviews were used to validate the subsystem. At the system level, documents should exist which summarize the inspection status of a document that, for example, seven out of ten subsystem designs have been reviewed and three have been developed but not yet been reviewed.

It is important that all the procedures which direct staff to sign-off an item that has been validated insist that the identification of the items as having been either tested or reviewed is modified at the same time. An excerpt from such a procedure is shown here, referring to the actions taken after a design review has taken place:

There will be three outcomes from a design review. First, the design, or more usually part of a design, will be passed as being correct; that is, no errors have been found. Second, small errors will have been found. In this case the chair of the review shall examine the corrected design and check that these small errors have been rectified; the design is then regarded as correct. Third, the design contains major errors. In this case the member of staff responsible for the design has to rectify the errors and re-present the item for further review.

In the first two cases the chair of the review will sign-off the design and update the configuration identity of the design to show that it has met its functional requirements. This is achieved simply by adding a capital letter M to the identity. The designer will then submit the design to the project library and it will normally come under configuration control. Staff who have a responsibility for the project library will check that both the identification of the design and the name of the file containing the design have been updated to show that it meets its functional requirements.

13.4 RELATION TO ISO 9000-3

The related section in ISO 9000-3 is Section 6.1. This describes the facilities that a configuration management system should offer. One of these is configuration identification, which refers to the discipline of recording the status of all configuration items. It states:

> The supplier should establish and maintain procedures for identifying software items during all phases, starting from specification through development, replication and delivery.

A component of this identification should describe whether the item at present conforms to requirements. Subsection 6.1.3.3 reiterates the fact that the suppliers should have some scheme for identifying configuration items:

> The supplier should establish and maintain procedures to record, manage and report on the status of software items, of change requests and of the implementation of approved changes.

13.5 PROBLEMS

The problems which are encountered if this part of the standard is not adhered to are:

* Modules are integrated into a system which have not been fully tested. This will result in errors being inserted which will require more resource to detect than if they were discovered during the programming task.
* Work is started on a system design based on a requirements specification that has not been adequately checked out.
* Work is started on programming based on designs which have not been adequately checked out.
* Not enough information is available to the project manager to allow him or her to track progress on validation.

13.6 CHECKS

The main check is that for every project the documentation standards adopted should insist that the test status of every configuration item and modules, if they are not configuration items, can be easily found by development staff and the project manager.

14

CONTROL OF NONCONFORMING PRODUCT

14.1 INTRODUCTION

The term *nonconforming product* refers to program code or documentation which does not currently conform to its requirements, or has not yet been validated and demonstrated that it meets requirements. Examples include modules which have not yet been tested, designs which have been reviewed and in which errors have been discovered but not yet rectified and systems which have been released to the customer in which customer staff have discovered a problem. This part of the standard concerns the release of items to the customer which are currently nonconforming:

> The supplier shall establish and maintain procedures to ensure that product that does not conform to specified requirements is prevented from inadvertent use or installation. Control shall provide for identification, documentation, evaluation, segregation (when practical), disposition of nonconforming product and for notification to the functions concerned.

There is one implication within this part of the standard which sits uneasily with current practice. When an engineered product such as a hair dryer is found to be defective, then there is often a mass recall of this item. However, with non-serious errors in software there is no direct example of this happening: the supplier does not usually send out a new version of a system when a customer discovers a non-threatening error. However, serious errors are dealt with in a similar way to engineered products with the supplier immediately allocating staff to the process of rectifying the error and new versions being sent out immediately.

14.2 NONCONFORMING PRODUCT DURING DEVELOPMENT

A large number of items make up a software system including modules, the requirements specification, the system design and test plans. Normally, the term 'nonconforming product' is assumed to refer to the program code and user manual as these are the items which will be delivered to the purchaser. However, there is a subtle implication in the standard that internal documents such as designs should be regarded as conforming or nonconforming as the excerpt above refers to 'inadvertent use'. This could mean inadvertent use of an internal document such as a design which has not been fully validated by a programmer.

Each module is programmed and tested by a programmer and deposited in the project library. At the point that the code has been tested and deposited in the library it can be regarded as conforming to requirements. A user manual is normally a configuration item. It is usually reviewed by a series of technical reviews and when the final section is checked it is normally baselined. After baselining it is regarded as having conformed to requirements. Subsystems are regarded as being conforming items after the acceptance tests associated with them have been completed

The implication from this part of the standard is that some form of documentation should be used to indicate the status of these items. For program modules the test status described in the previous chapter would be adequate. This forms part of the comments normally included in the header of the module.

For the user manual a cover sheet for each section should indicate its review status: whether it is awaiting review, whether it has been reviewed and errors have been discovered which have not been rectified or whether the section has been signed-off as being correct.

For subsystems and the system itself a simple item of documentation which details the progress of the acceptance tests would be adequate. This form of documentation would normally have to be produced in order to conform to the part of the standard which deals with test and inspection status.

For internal documents such as a system design, a cover sheet for each component of the document—in the case of the system design, subsystem designs—should indicate the status of the item: whether it has been validated or not.

As well as this documentation there is a need for procedures to be followed which instruct staff to check on the status of modules and subsystems which are to be integrated into the final system, and which also instruct staff to make manual checks on the covers and the sections of the user manual to ensure that sections which have not been checked or which still have errors will not be included in a printed version of the manual.

There is also the implication in this section of the standard that if errors are detected during the later stages of the testing process, i.e. during integration, system or acceptance testing, then procedures should be in place to feed back information about the detection of errors to staff responsible for rectifying the errors so that they can discover the cause.

It is important that the quality system provides a standard for summary documentation which describes the state of a project in terms of nonconforming product, and procedures which enable that documentation to be easily updated. The form of this documentation is usually simple: it consists of a list of modules and subsystems together with their status and, possibly, information about what actions are currently being carried out in order to make the product conforming.

14.3 ERRORS DURING OPERATION

It is important to point out that the previous section has concentrated on conformity being demonstrated during the validation of a phase product, for example as part of the module testing process. Another area where errors are detected and which affects the status of software occurs when a phase discovers problems or errors that should have been picked up in a previous phase.

14.4 RELATION TO ISO 9000-3

The relevant parts of ISO 9000-3 are Sections 5.6, 5.7, 5.9 and 6.1. The final part of Section 5.6 states that:

> The supplier shall carry out reviews to ensure that the requirements are met and the above methods are correctly carried out. The design or implementation process should not proceed until the consequences of all known deficiencies are satisfactorily resolved or the risk of proceeding otherwise is known. *Records of such reviews should be maintained.*

I have italicized the most relevant part which directs the supplier to ensure that the outcome of a review can be easily determined and hence whether an item which has been reviewed can be discovered to be currently conforming or nonconforming.

Section 5.7 concerns testing. The relevance of this section is that it directs the supplier to document test results and also to any problems that have been encountered during testing.

Section 5.9 concerns the replication, delivery and installation of the software product. Here, Subsection 5.9.2 states that:

> Provisions should be made for verifying the correctness and completeness of copies of the software product delivered.

The implication here is that some form of check that nonconforming product is not delivered should be incorporated.

Section 6.1 concerns configuration management. Subsection 6.1.3.3 directs the supplier to document the status of configuration items. Part of the status information will be whether an item is conforming or nonconforming.

14.5 PROBLEMS

The main problem that this part of the standard is intended to address is of product or user documentation being released to the purchaser or to system and acceptance testing staff which has not been properly validated. If your quality system is weak in this respect, then there will be a high number of error reports generated during system and acceptance testing or a high level of purchaser problems detected during operation. Normally a good configuration management system satisfies the requirements of this part of the standard.

14.6 CHECKS

* Standards and procedures exist for the identification of modules as conforming or nonconforming.
* Standards and procedures exist for the identification of user manuals as conforming or nonconforming.
* Standards and procedures exist for the identification of internal documents such as system designs and requirements specifications as conforming or nonconforming.
* Standards for acceptance testing and system testing include documentation which can be consulted to determine the status of subsystems or the overall system.
* Standards are in place which allow staff to quickly discern what the state of a project is in terms of the number of items which are conforming and nonconforming.
* Procedures exist which instruct staff who discover errors during validation to flag the items that caused the error to be marked as nonconforming.
* Procedures exist which instruct staff to check on the status of all the items which make up a software system before release to the purchaser.
* Procedures exist which instruct staff to check on the status of the user manual before it is released to the purchaser.

15

CORRECTIVE ACTION

15.1 INTRODUCTION

This section of the standard describes what a software developer should do when a problem is notified which gives rise to nonconforming product. That is, the supplier shall have procedures for:

> Investigating the cause of nonconforming product and the corrective actions needed to prevent recurrence.

and

> Applying controls to ensure that corrective actions are taken and they are effective.

Examples of this include the detection of errors in system testing which arise because of an error committed by a programmer who developed a particular module, or the detection by the customer during operation of an error which arose from a design defect.

This part of the standard deals with what should happen when these defects are discovered and what actions the software developer should take in order to minimize the incidence of defects. In this respect this part of the standard is intimately connected with many of the concerns which lie at the heart of the revision and maintenance of a company's quality system.

15.2 CORRECTIVE FEEDBACK LOOPS

When an error is discovered by developmental staff or by the customer there should be well-defined procedures in existence which govern what should happen next. Normally these procedures will be the same from project to project, and will involve a series of tasks:

- The aberrant behaviour of the system, or part of the system, which is being validated is detailed in some form of error-reporting documentation.
- ·If the defect arose from a customer report, then the defect is checked out by another member of staff who attempts to replicate the problem. This member of staff determines whether, in fact, an error was detected. This is particularly important since these 'defects' may have arisen because the customer has not properly read the user manual, or may even represent an attempt to force the developer to include some extra functionality under the guise of an error.
- If the reported problem was an error then the member of staff who confirms this fact then notifies a senior member of staff—usually a senior programmer—who will then allocate staff to eliminate the error.
- Notification of a proposed change to remedy the error is sent to the change control board who would normally give permission to proceed.
- The error is rectified and a series of tests carried out to ensure that the change to the program code has not affected other parts of the system.
- A new version of the software item is created and documented in the quality system and new documentation is circulated to developmental staff who are affected by the change.

A good quality system should have a well-defined route from the detection of an error to the configuration management system adopted for a project. There should also be a route from the detection of errors to the eventual process of improving the quality system.

15.3 DEFECT ANALYSIS

This part of the standard is also concerned with the fact that the developer should be continually monitoring error reports and problems experienced in the field in order to eliminate problems with the quality system. All incidents of defects which give rise to non-conforming software should be documented in a project defect log. This defect log would contain some reference to a unique identifier which identifies the error documentation that describes the detected error, a reason for the error, and an indicator which gives some assessment of whether the cause of the error was sufficiently serious to take immediate action by modifying the quality system. When a mature quality system is being used, the type of errors which give rise to immediate modification to that system are usually those which apply to some new project-specific standards and procedures. For example, a project may be the first to employ a particular programming language, and part of the quality plan for the project involves a programming standard which is not immediately added to the quality system. This standard may have some problems which give rise to certain categories of error that are detected during integration testing. If the project manager thinks that these errors are sufficiently serious, then he or she may order a modification of the standard.

Tips and techniques 24

Often, it is impractical for a supplier to monitor every error which has been detected in a project in order to construct a database that enables the quality system to be reviewed. I normally advise developers to concentrate on using technical reviews as a medium for documenting the level of errors that were detected by a project, particularly if code reviews are used. As long as something like 40% of the reviews are used to generate error data, then the developer will have a good idea of the strengths and weaknesses of their quality system.

It is important that any changes are recorded and the version-numbering conventions applied to the quality system are respected. Normally changes which are initiated by a particular project result in a minor version number of the quality system being adjusted. For example, a change to a programming standard would mean the quality system which had a version number of 1.3 would have a version number of 1.4.

Often, though, the error logs that are produced by a project are stored and used in the next cycle of revision to the quality system. The ISO 9001 standard is very firm on the need for a quality system to be revised periodically. When a quality system is revised there are a number of sources of information which are used to guide this revision. They include: suggestions from project staff elicited via quality circles or suggestion boxes; reports from the R & D department or consultants on the impact of new technology; business policy statements by senior management; and post-mortems from projects which have underachieved.

A major input into the process of quality system improvement is the defect log which describes errors that have been detected on projects. Normally this information is given to staff charged with quality system improvement in a summary form. For example, defects due to programming might be displayed as summary data showing the number of defects within a certain seriousness category and displayed according to the programming language standard used.

It is worth stressing in conclusion that a quality system should not only be documenting defects which arise from programming but also defects which arise from other developmental activities such as system design, requirements analysis, project costing and test planning.

15.4 RELATION TO ISO 9000-3

Section 4.4 of ISO 9000-3 is a duplication of the corresponding section in the ISO 9001 standard.

15.5 PROBLEMS

The problems which are encountered if this part of the standard is not adhered to are:

- Inadequate procedures governing the feedback of information from staff who have detected problems. These give rise to errors not being rectified, or too much effort being spent discovering what the error was that needed to be addressed.
- Inadequate procedures and standards governing the interface between staff who detect errors and staff responsible for configuration management. These give rise to errors not being notified to the project and inadequate validation of the changes which address those errors which have been notified.
- Poor information from the analysis of defects leads to important information not being used by staff charged with improving the quality system. This results in the quality system evolving less efficiently than it might if the information was available.

15.6 CHECKS

- Standards exist which govern the nature and layout of information generated when an error is detected.
- Project planning procedures exist which enable the project manager to define the interface between the configuration management system used on a project and the staff charged with validation.
- Procedures exist for immediate feedback from projects to the quality system when a serious deficiency in a component of the system is detected.
- Guidelines exist which detail how information from the validation process can be used by staff who are charged with the improvement of the quality system.
- A standard exists which describes the nature of the information to be included in a project's defect log and procedures exist which detail how that log is updated.

16

HANDLING, STORAGE, PACKAGING AND DELIVERY

16.1 INTRODUCTION

This rather innocuous part of the quality standard describes a number of important points concerned with the delivery of the software product and its subsequent fate:

> The supplier shall establish, document and maintain procedures for handling, storage, packaging and delivery of product.

Although this part of the standard seems to be mainly concerned with items such as warehousing there are, intertwined within it, a number of concerns about adequate storage of project documents together with concerns about purchaser support.

16.2 PROJECT DOCUMENTS

It is important that every project builds a project library. The quality system should describe the documentation numbering and identification conventions that are used for items which have been consigned to this library. These conventions usually consist of some form of identifier which describes what the item is, the name of the item, its version number and the date that it was deposited in the project library. For example the designator *DD1.3 SS1 Startup 10.12.92* would describe a detailed design (*DD*) called *Startup* which has a version number 1.3 and was deposited in the library on the 10th December 1992. The identity of these items should be prominently displayed on their cover sheet and on the head of each page. Normally the project library will be divided into directories, subdirectories and sub-subdirectories which reflect the structure of the documentation. For example, there would be directories for subsystems which would be split up into subdirectories for designs, subdirectories for the program code of modules, and so on.

The project library should be organized so that all staff have read access but very few have write access. Indeed, it is worth having write access confined to whoever acts as the project librarian. This person would normally interface with staff who are carrying out the configuration management role and would only enter new items into the library or modify existing items if the full procedures associated with either establishing a baseline or validating a change to a baseline have been carried out. Part of a procedure for inserting items into a project library is:

> Each project will maintain a project library whose structure is described in Section 4.5.6 of this quality manual. The project will nominate a project librarian who will be the only person who will have write access to the library. The library will contain all major project documentation and also all program code. The documentation it will contain will be the requirements specification, system design, detailed design of all subsystems, system test plan and acceptance test plan. If a change has been applied to an item in the project library, then the new version of the item that has been changed will need to be presented to the librarian with evidence that the change has been sanctioned together with the validation records that indicate that the change has been checked and that no other parts of the system have been affected by the change. The project librarian will update the version number of the item, delete the previous version and issue an update note to the project that a new version of the item has been inserted.

16.3 SAFE STORAGE

The standard specifies that documents and program code should be adequately stored. The implication here is that the storage procedures adopted by the company should guard against a number of serious problems occurring. The first is natural disaster: events such as flooding or fire. This requires backup of all project documents at regular intervals, preferably to fire-proof safes or remote locations.

A modern form of disaster which the software supplier should guard against is that of viruses. Normally, regular backups cope with the majority of viruses. However, there are some viruses which do not announce themselves in direct ways and which subtly modify source files and object files over a period of time. This means that the software supplier may carry out a number of backups which gradually result in files becoming more and more corrupt without anyone noticing. The solution is to have procedures which result in the application of file comparison tools over a period of time.

Procedures should also be used which regularly check the file amendment data on each item in the project library against the date of last modification. Any mismatches might indicate some viral infection or a lapse in the procedures governing the access of staff to the project library. For example, a member of staff could, quite legally, amend a subsystem but have forgotten to amend the date associated with the subsystem.

16.4 THE RELEASE OF WRONG CODE OR DOCUMENTATION

Another concern here is that it should not be possible to release the wrong document or program code to staff on a project or the purchaser. There are two implications.

The first implication is that there should be some procedures which govern the release of items from the project library. For example, the release of an item has to be accompanied by a form which details the item to be read from the library, with the issue of the item being carried out in such a way that the librarian has to document the precise details of the item released.

Tips and techniques 25

There is scope for the use of simple tools which assemble and check that the right code configuration has been released to the purchaser. A release note can be prepared which can be keyed into a file. This file would contain the version numbers and other release information for each of the components of a system. A very simple tool could be written which then examines the version information maintained by an operating system together with any information which is mandatory for the development team to include in the file names of the components, and assembles the system described by the release note. The development of such a tool can be carried out in a matter of days; with an operating system such as UNIX in a matter of hours.

The second implication is that there should be procedures which check that the correct system is being released to the purchaser. This is normally very simple to achieve. If the supplier was developing a system for one purchaser it normally involves staff charged with releasing the system checking that an up-to-date version was sent out. When a number of purchasers are involved, where each received a tailored version of the software, the procedure would be a little more time consuming, although essentially the same as that adopted when issuing a whole system. The procedures adopted for a project should result in a build in terms of modules and version numbers of modules being specified, normally after a purchaser has ordered a particular version of the software. The staff charged with this activity should be guided by procedures which ask them to check version information and module names of the system to be released. For large systems this can be done automatically by a simple software tool which can be developed in-house.

16.5 POST DELIVERY SERVICE

While this book has stressed the development of a quality plan for delivery there is a further quality plan which project managers have to develop:

> The supplier shall arrange for the protection of the quality of product after final inspection and test. Where contractually specified, this protection shall be extended to include delivery to destination.

This is the plan that governs what is to happen after the project software has been delivered. Normally a software supplier who produces bespoke software will sign some form of maintenance contract. This contract will specify the level of support to be expected from the supplier, how problems are to be communicated to the supplier and conditions such as the fact that certain categories of error are to be rectified within a particular time. It is the role of the project manager, in consultation with staff who are to carry out purchaser support, to produce a quality plan which details how this support is to be implemented.

This means that for post-development support the project manager should be able to draw upon standards which deal with the documents which are to be filled in when the purchaser discovers errors from the field, documents which have to be communicated from staff who are supporting the software to staff who are maintaining it, documents which summarize the current state of the system in terms of outstanding errors, summary documents which describe the number and severity of errors notified from the field together with the proportion of reports which actually turned out to be errors, and release documentation for each version of the system.

The amount of documentation that is needed by a project manager will vary from project to project and will depend on the support contract that was signed. For example, the software supplier may have signed a contract which guarantees that reported errors of a certain severity will be rectified within a certain time period. For this the supplier needs some form of document interchange between staff fielding the error and the supplier which agrees an error either is of the specified severity or is not.

As well as standards, there is a need for procedures which govern the actions that are to be taken by staff fielding reported errors from the purchaser. Most of these procedures will involve the process of filling in forms, for example to notify the maintenance staff of an error, but may also involve asking the purchaser to run diagnostic tests.

16.6 RELATION TO ISO 9000-3

The relevant parts of ISO 9000-3 are Sections 5.8 and 5.9. Section 5.8 concerns acceptance of the product and details the fact that some form of acceptance testing should occur and that the quality plan should specify how anomalies detected during acceptance should be detailed:

> When the supplier is ready to deliver the validated product, the purchaser should judge whether or not the product is acceptable according to previously agreed criteria and in a manner specified in the contract.
> The method of handling problems detected during the acceptance procedure and their disposition should be agreed between the purchaser and the supplier and should be documented.

Section 5.9 deals with replication, delivery and installation. Subsection 5.9.1 instructs the supplier to pay attention to issues such as the delivery of documentation including manuals, disaster recovery plans, the form of media used for distribution and the period in which the supplier is obliged to issue copies of the delivered software.

Subsection 5.9.2 makes the point that some form of correctness checking should be made between what is planned to be delivered to the purchaser and what is assembled on some delivery medium such as a floppy disk.

Subsection 5.9.3 makes the point that the roles and responsibilities of both the supplier and the purchaser should be clearly specified when considering installation. For example, who is to be responsible for the installation, who is to be responsible for checking that the correct installation has occurred, what facilities are to be offered to the supplier's staff who are to carry out installation and how agreement over correct installation is to be reached.

16.7 PROBLEMS

The problems which are encountered if this part of the standard is not adhered to are:

- Time is wasted in looking for poorly identified documents.
- Documents which have been baselined are updated in an unorganized manner. This leads to errors by staff using these documents because circulated documents such as the system design may not be up to date.
- Valuable project documents are destroyed or lost because of circumstances such as fire.
- Software is destroyed or degraded due to virus attack.
- Systems are released to the purchaser which contain wrong components.
- Inadequate communication between staff who are supporting purchasers and staff who are maintaining a system.
- Inadequate communication between the purchaser and staff involved in support.

16.8 CHECKS

- Project planning standards exist which describe the form of a project library.
- Numbering conventions are included in standards for all the main documents and code produced by a project.
- Procedures exist which restrict access to the project library.
- Procedures exist which describe the safe storage of both project documents and program code.
- Standards exist which describe the various configurations that a software system may be released in.
- Procedures exist which direct staff to check that the configuration of a released system matches the configuration which was specified to be released.
- Standards exist which govern the communication between staff who carry out the support function and the maintenance function.
- Standards exist which govern the communication between staff charged with support and staff charged with maintenance.
- Standards exist which govern the communication between the purchaser and the staff who carry out support.
- Guidelines exist which help the project manager decide on a quality plan for support, given that the software supplier will have signed a contract for support—often at the same time as the contract for development.
- Procedures and standards exist which enable staff charged with support to generate statistics on the level and severity of the errors notified by the purchaser.

17

QUALITY RECORDS

17.1 INTRODUCTION

This part of the standard lies at the core of many of the important concerns that a software supplier should address concerning quality. It is about the maintenance of quality records:

> The supplier shall establish and maintain procedures for identification, collection, indexing, filing, storage, maintenance and disposition of quality records.

Quality records are documentation which provide assurance that certain quality factors are present in the system to be developed:

> Quality records shall be maintained to demonstrate achievement of the required quality and the effective operation of the quality system. Pertinent subcontractor quality records shall be an element of these data.

In Chapter 1 I described the fact that the main function of a quality system is to ensure that a delivered system contains certain quality factors which have been identified by the project manager at the beginning of a project—often this identification is done in concert with staff from the quality assurance function and, of course, the purchaser.

Chapter 1 described a number of these quality factors including correctness, interoperability, portability and maintainability. It is the responsibility of the project manager to identify these factors based on discussions with the purchaser and purchaser-generated documents. For example, if the purchaser has specified that the portability quality factor is to be high, as evidenced by a wish that the system to be developed should be capable of running on a wide variety of operating systems, then the quality plan should specify validation activities which demonstrate that portability is present and which gives rise to documentation that can be audited to ensure that the validation activities have been carried out. For example, staff who carry out the portability testing should run duplicate sets of tests for each target operating system and generate test records which show that each functional test has been carried out and correctly executed. Another example would be where staff carry out a check that portability is ensured in a developed system by processing the source code with a tool which details any deviations from an ANSI standard. Here the quality record that demonstrates that the validation has taken place will be the printout from the tool.

17.2 QUALITY PLANNING

A quality system which is of an ISO 9001 standard should provide guidelines for the project manager which enable him or her to elicit the quality factors that are important for a particular project. Almost invariably, functional correctness will always be required: the system does what the requirements specification specifies it should do. However, there will be a number of quality factors such as portability and interoperability which will depend on the application and a purchaser's particular circumstances.

The quality system should also specify standards and procedures which govern the development of the quality plan. This is a document which details how the quality factors identified at the beginning of a project will be validated. It is similar to any other plan, in that it will contain: a specification of tasks; designation of staff to carry out the tasks; resources, both hardware and software, to carry out the tasks; and the temporal relationship between tasks, for example whether one task has to follow another or whether tasks can be carried out in parallel with others. The only difference between this plan and the developmental plan will be that the activities it describes will all be oriented towards demonstrating the presence of quality factors. Typical activities which it will describe are:

- The application of a series of tests which check that a particular functional requirement has been correctly implemented.
- The application of a standard test set across versions of a system targeted at a number of hardware platforms in order to check that there is no variability between the different implementations.
- The calculation of the reliability of a system by examining the results from testing in terms of the number of errors discovered, and when they were discovered during the system testing phase.
- The checking of a module by a code review for the absence of features which lead to poor maintainability. This activity is normally only one component of a code review, but is an important one if the supplier perceives that the maintenance quality factor needs to be high in a delivered system.

In the quality plan there should also be a description of any supporting activities which need to be executed in order that the validation activities above can be carried out. Two examples of such tasks are the preparation of data files for performance testing and the development of a testing tool which enables staff to track the statement coverage of test data.

The standards for the quality plan should specify the form of the structure of the plan, the quality controls which are to be used on the project which the plan describes and the way in which individual tasks are described and their relationship to other quality tasks and developmental tasks.

There should be procedures which specify how the quality plan is developed and how it is validated. Normally the validation is achieved by means of some technical review, although for small projects a check by a senior manager with a consequent signing-off of the document is normally adequate.

17.3 QUALITY RECORDS

This part of the standard is clear about quality records: that where components of a quality factor are validated, then the documentation which demonstrates that the validation has been carried out and was successful should be easily identified and should be capable of being easily retrieved. For example, if the project manager, or even the purchaser, wishes to check the quality records which cover the functional correctness of part of a system, then it should be easy for those records to be retrieved from the project's archives. This means some form of identification convention for the records should be specified and adhered to by a project. There will normally be two forms of identification. First, there will be a unique identifier which distinguishes the quality record from other quality records. Part of this identifier may include some form of designation which describes what type of quality record it is: whether, for example, it is a record which provides assurance that certain aspects of a systems response time are correct, or whether a check has been made that some programming standard which encourages maintenance has been adhered to.

The second form of identification enforces traceability. The vast majority of the quality records generated by a project will refer to particular properties of the system detailed in the requirements specification. There should be some back reference to the part of the requirements specification which gave rise to the quality record. For example, if in the requirements specification there was a statement that the response time of a certain command was x seconds, this will be identified uniquely in the requirements specification and the quality record which checks this out—normally some test report— should reference this unique identifier.

Quality records will exist in a number of forms. Some examples of the variety of quality records that can be generated by a project are:

- Test reports which check that functions specified in the requirements specification have been implemented correctly.
- The minutes of reviews. Normally these reviews cover both functional and non-functional correctness together with a consideration of whether the item being reviewed conforms to the standards adopted by the project.
- The documentation generated when one programmer walks through an item such as a programmed module in the presence of the programmer who coded the module.
- The printout from a tool. For example, the supplier may have bought a tool which applies software metrics to the design of the system. Such metrics often give a good indication of the maintainability of a system and the project manager may have

decided that since the maintainability quality factor should be high for a particular system, then no module should have a numeric complexity higher than a certain figure. The printout from the tool, after it has been applied to a design, would be the quality record which indicates that the maintainability quality factor was high.

- Printouts from operating system utilities. For example a printout which indicates that a system has satisfied certain memory requirements.

- A report from a set of usability tests which indicate that a low level of user errors has been encountered in running the system with a particular interface. This would be a quality record which indicates that the usability quality factor was high in the system.

Such quality records should be generated by both the supplier and any subcontractors who are used on a project, and should be easily accessible to both project management and the staff who carry out the quality function. It is important that the quality records are retained for a period after the software project has been completed. It is also important that they be stored for a period which has been agreed between the supplier and the purchaser.

17.4 TESTING DOCUMENTATION

Before concluding this chapter it is worth describing an important category of documentation which gives rise to the vast majority of quality records on a software project: the documentation associated with testing.

At the beginning of the software project a requirements specification will be generated which will describe both the functional and non-functional properties of a system. At an early stage in the software project staff charged with system and acceptance testing will take this document and generate a list of outline tests; these are often known as *verification requirements*. These form the foundation for the detailed tests which will be carried out at the end of the project.

During the software project the staff charged with system and acceptance testing will produce a test design specification. This will describe, for each related set of verification requirements, how a series of tests will be carried out. For example, a personnel system may have a series of functional requirements concerned with the retrieval of data related to the training of staff. A test design would specify how those verification requirements relevant to these group of functions will be tested: what test software will be needed; what test database will be required; what hardware base will be needed; in what order the tests will be carried out; whether some tests need to be carried out before others; and so on.

The test design then gives rise to test specifications and test procedures. The former describe each test in more detail, while the latter are a step-by-step description of how to carry out a test. Often these two documents are combined together.

The outcome of each test will be documented in a test report. Test reports can be written for each test that has been carried out or can cover a group of tests. The choice of which to adopt depends on the complexity of the tests that are to be applied. If simple tests are to be applied to a clerical system, then each test outcome document would cover a collection of tests; however, if a complex real-time system is to be tested, then each test will be associated with one item of documentation. The test outcome documentation represents the quality records for the project.

Tips and techniques 1

Always attempt to include a directive to your staff in test procedures which asks them to explain why they have chosen certain test data. This is of most value in procedures governing unit and integration testing which are relatively informal processes. For example, there are three main testing strategies used for generating test data: normal data derivation, error guessing and boundary data generation. The first, normal data derivation, is the construction of well-behaved test data. The second involves the development of test data which is, in a sense, in error; for example, floating point data for a command which expects integer or string data. The third is the development of data which lies on the boundary of two functions. For example, a command may carry out one function if a parameter is less than 200 and another function if the parameter is greater or equal to 200; in this case a test value of 200 should be used for the parameter.

A piece of documentation which is generated towards the end of a project is the test summary report. This report normally covers each subsystem and represents a summary of the tests which have been applied to the subsystem. It will specify how many tests have been applied to a subsystem, how many tests have been successful, how many have been unsuccessful and the degree to which they have been unsuccessful; whether, for example, a test was an outright failure or whether some of the expected results of the test actually occurred.

Most of the tests that are applied to a system will be functional; however, some of the tests will be non-functional, for example a test that file-size restrictions have been adhered to. The test documentation which has been detailed here has mainly concerned system and acceptance testing. It is important that a project follows standards for both unit testing and integration testing. The former would describe the data that was used for a module test, the strategy used for generating the data, the test outcomes, and the test software and hardware employed. The documentation for integration testing would be similar to this, but would also include details of which build of a system was tested.

1.5 RELATION TO ISO 9000-3

The part of ISO 9000-3 which is relevant to this topic, Section 6.3, is merely a restatement of the ISO 9001 section; nothing more is added.

17.6 PROBLEMS

The problems which are encountered if this part of the standard is not adhered to are:

- An incoherent quality plan is produced which may result in many validation activities not being carried out at all, some validation activities being carried out inefficiently and other validation activities being only partially executed.
- A poor quality plan not giving the project manager enough indication of the level of resources—hardware, software and staff—required for validation. This either leads to too many staff being allocated to validation or too few.
- Inadequate quality records are generated. This means that both project management and the purchaser would have great difficulty discovering whether a system had been adequately validated.
- A poor quality plan is produced which leads to inadequate quality controls being associated with the project.
- Poorly specified test documentation which results in not enough information being given to testers and almost certainly leads to tests being poorly carried out.
- Poor testing standards which result in inadequate coverage of the functional and non-functional properties of a system during acceptance and system testing.
- Poor module testing and integration testing standards which result in a system being sent to the system and acceptance testers that still have major errors. This results in an increased level of resource required for these activities.

17.7 CHECKS

- Guidelines exist which provide advice to the project manager on constructing a quality plan.
- Standards exist which specify the form of the quality plan.
- Procedures exist which govern the construction and development of the quality plan.
- Standards exist for all the documents generated by quality control-based activities such as technical reviews.
- Procedures exist for the conduct of all activities associated with quality controls.
- Standards exist for all testing documentation including verification requirements, test designs, test specifications, test procedures and test reports.
- Procedures exist that result in subcontractors producing similar quality records to those produced on the project that uses the subcontractors. These procedures could be included in those which relate to the process of contracting subcontractors.

INTERNAL QUALITY AUDITS

18.1 INTRODUCTION

An internal quality audit of a project is a visit to that project carried out by staff charged with quality assurance. The visit is intended to check that the quality controls embedded in the quality plan have been carried out by staff on the project. Typically such staff might check that:

- All changes during a certain period have been processed by the configuration management system.
- A project manager has adhered to the standards describing how the developmental plan for the project should be detailed.
- A programmer has carried out the detailed procedures associated with module programming and testing. For example, that he or she has stored test data away in a file and that the name of the file conforms to the conventions that are specified in the quality manual.
- All technical reviews within a certain planned period have occurred and have been signed off by the chair of each review.

There are two reasons why auditing is carried out. The first and, sadly, the most important reason is to act as a check that a project is following the agreed controls that are described in its project plan. This is vital for companies which have been certified to an ISO 9001 standard since any major deviations from a project plan detected by external auditors from the certifying body could easily result in the ISO certification being withdrawn. Indeed, it is often said that getting certification, although fairly tough in terms of the amount of work required to develop procedures and standards, is nothing like the difficulty in keeping certification by means of ensuring that projects respect quality controls. This part of the role of internal auditing involves quality staff acting as policemen.

The second reason for auditing arises from the fact that results from internal auditing are a useful input into the process of improving the quality system. There are a number of reasons why staff do not respect quality controls: in my experience the main one is a desire to produce a software system on time and to budget with the quality system being seen as a brake on that process. However, another reason for quality controls being ignored or only partially followed is that there may be something wrong with a part of the quality system which is associated with some quality controls.

The reasons for auditing are summed up in the standard:

> The supplier shall carry out a comprehensive system of planned and documented quality audits to verify whether quality activities comply with planned arrangements and to determine the effectiveness of the quality system.

A good example of auditing pinpointing problems in a quality system occurs where a programming standard for a new programming language might have been recently introduced and an audit on a number of projects discovered that quite a few programmers have violated the standard. In carrying out a post-mortem it might be discovered that certain features of the standard militate against the production of efficient code and need to be modified. In auditing, internal quality staff should always be aware of this reason for non-compliance with the standards and procedures associated with a project.

18.2 THE PROCESS OF AUDITING

A good quality system should provide advice on how to plan for the auditing process on a project. This advice is normally enshrined in auditing guidelines. There are a number of aspects of auditing which these guidelines address.

The first is when internal audits should take place. It is normal practice to carry out an audit after some major event has happened on a project. Typical major events would include the development of the first draft of the project plan, the baselining of the requirements specification, the baselining of the system design and the completion of the system tests. These audit points would be described in the quality plan.

Many software suppliers also carry out audits with no warning given to the project team. Such audits, often known as spot-checks, should be guided by the project plan. For example, it is no use carrying out a series of spot-checks on the finished code of a system unless the project has passed the point where quite a few of the modules in the system have been programmed and tested. Since this form of audit is heavily guided by the project plan it acts as an extra check that the project is actually running on time. If quality staff turn up to spot-check an activity and discover that activity has not been completed, even though the latest version of the project plan states that the activity should have terminated, then this fact should be conveyed to the manager who the project manager reports to.

The next aspect which auditing guidelines need to address is what to audit. There is never enough resource to audit everything on a software project and staff charged with the auditing task need to be selective. Normally the policy taken in auditing is to examine important components of the project such as the project plan and the requirements specification and only to audit items such as modules on an occasional basis:

Audits shall be scheduled on the basis of the status and importance of the activity.

There are some exceptions to this. For example, a member of staff may, in the past, have had a record of non-compliance with the agreed quality controls of a project and a high-level decision might be made to audit their work on a more frequent basis than might normally be so. Also, it is often a good idea to audit the work of new staff a little more frequently, in order to check that they have understood the nature of the standards and procedures that they have to work with. It also provides solid evidence to new members of staff of the seriousness with which a company takes its quality system.

18.3 NON-COMPLIANCE

One of the most important parts of a software quality system is that concerned with the reporting of the results of an audit and the actions that may have to be taken when an audit reports non-compliance. Standards and procedures should exist for reporting on the result of an audit. In general, for minor infringements, the project manager concerned will be notified, although summary data detailing the extent of these infringements will normally be passed up to whoever manages the quality system and the manager who the project manager reports to. Serious infringements will be notified to the next level of management up and will normally result in some form of high-level reprimand.

In general there will be two sorts of non-compliance: serious and minor. An example of a minor non-compliance occurs where a programmer does not follow the conventions for naming identifiers in a module. A serious non-compliance occurs where a requirements specification is given to the system designers without it being fully reviewed.

The quality system should have standards which describe the form of the information which emerges from an audit. As well as bureaucratic information such as the name of the project which was audited, the date of the audit and what was examined, it should also summarize the extent of any non-compliances that were discovered.

The procedures which will be adopted when non-compliance is discovered should be detailed in the quality plan for a project. The quality plan should also detail what follow-up actions should be taken when a non-compliance is discovered. This normally would direct the project manager to check that the task which was audited is carried out correctly; when the task is an important one, such as the specification of an important subsystem, there may even be a requirement to re-audit the whole process.

18.4 RELATION TO ISO 9000-3

The part of ISO 9000-3 which is relevant to this topic, Section 4.3, is merely a restatement of the ISO 9001 section; nothing more is added.

18.5 PROBLEMS

The problems which are encountered if this part of the standard is not adhered to are:

- Poor or infrequent auditing results in projects not adhering to the agreed quality controls. This normally results in software which contains errors and which does not meet purchaser requirements.
- Poor auditing leads to staff perceiving a lack of importance of quality in a company.
- Inadequate auditing removes a useful technique for external checking on the progress of a project.
- Poor or non-existent auditing leads to valuable information which could be used to improve the quality system and improve developmental tasks being lost.

18.6 CHECKS

- Guidelines exist which inform quality staff when and what to audit in a project.
- Procedures exist which describe how an audit is to take place.
- Procedures exist which describe how a spot-check is to take place.
- Standards exist which describe the documentation generated by an audit or a spot-check.
- Procedures for quality planning describe how audit points are identified and how they are documented in the quality plan.
- Procedures exist which detail the steps that are to be taken when a minor infringement is discovered during an audit or a spot-check.
- Procedures exist which detail the steps that are to be taken when a major infringement is discovered during an audit or a spot-check.

19

TRAINING

19.1 INTRODUCTION

This small part of the standard is about the training that a company gives its staff: how training needs are identified, how staff are allocated to projects based on training and work experience and how training records are kept:

> The supplier shall establish and maintain procedures for identifying the training needs and provide for the training of all personnel performing activities affecting quality. Personnel performing specific assigned tasks shall be qualified on the basis of appropriate education, training and/or experience, as required. Appropriate records of training shall be maintained.

19.2 ASSESSING COMPANY TRAINING NEEDS

As a minimum the company should institute a review of training needs on a yearly basis. This review would involve the training function, project management, high-level management and the marketing function. Input from the latter is very important as it can give a good idea of what commercial demands the outside world will place on the company over the coming years. There will be a number of inputs into the review of training needs:

- Reports from project managers on deficiencies found in certain common developmental tasks such as module testing.
- Reports on new market conditions which may necessitate application-specific training. For example, the marketing department may report that they see a large increase in business in the area of flexible manufacturing. If so, then the company may feel that some senior staff need training in this technology in order to talk sensibly to purchasers of software in this area.

- Reports on company strategy from senior management. For example, it may be envisaged that a high degree of automation is to be introduced into software projects over the near future. This would necessitate specific training in the tools that are to be purchased.
- Reports on the effectiveness of the quality system. Often such reports pinpoint poor execution of both managerial and technical tasks. Often, this poor performance can be eliminated by means of suitable training.

The review should be issued to all staff, who should be made aware of the training opportunities that it envisages.

19.3 THE MAINTENANCE OF TRAINING AND EXPERIENCE RECORDS

It is important that both the work experience and training of each member of staff in a company from the directors downward is kept. Normally the training records would include: what courses were attended; their nature, for example whether they were technical and specific such as a course which teaches how to use a particular tool, or general such as a course on testing; and a statement of the ways in which the course empowered the member of staff to carry out tasks which, in the past he or she could not do, or did suboptimally.

Tips and techniques 27

It is often a good idea to ask the member of staff who attended a course to write a brief report detailing how attendance would benefit the company. This report should be filed with the training record for that member of staff. Such reports are often a good source of criticism of current developmental and QA practices and can form a useful input into the process of revising the quality system.

The work experience record should detail the tasks carried out by the member of staff on the projects in which he or she worked, the nature of the system that was built on the project and a statement of any new skills which were learned as part of the work assignment.

It is an important principle that any firm which is certified to ISO 9001 should ensure that, during project planning, staff who are qualified and trained for a particular task are assigned to that task. At the very worst, companies who have to use a member of staff who is inexperienced or who has not received adequate training should ensure that training is provided before the task is started and that such staff are closely monitored.

19.4 ASSIGNMENT OF STAFF TO TASKS

Part of the planning process involves a project manager allocating staff to specific tasks on a project. The quality system should provide guidelines for the allocation of tasks together with some checklists which can be consulted to check that the right staff have been allocated. There should also be a short standard which describes how staff allocation details are displayed in the project plan. Often, at an early stage in a project, specific members of the project cannot be identified. In this case the project planning procedures and standards should insist that, as a minimum, the experience and expected training of the member of staff should be specified.

19.5 RELATION TO ISO 9000-3

ISO 9000-3 merely restates the principle that the supplier should identify training needs and makes the point, stressed in this chapter, that staff who carry out a task should be both experienced and have received adequate training to carry out that task. It briefly describes some of the areas to be addressed when considering training:

> The subjects to be addressed should be determined considering the specific tools, techniques, methodologies and computer resources to be used in the development and management of the software product. It might also be required to include the training of skills and knowledge of the specific field with which the software is to deal.

19.6 PROBLEMS

The problems which are encountered if this part of the standard is not adhered to are:

- Tasks are executed poorly because the staff allocated to a task are not adequately qualified to carry it out.
- The workforce of the company becomes gradually outdated in skills.
- The company is unable to tender in particular application areas because of a lack of knowledge of those areas.

19.7 CHECKS

- Guidelines exist which help the project manager allocate the most suitable staff to technical tasks.
- Guidelines exist which enable a company to determine its future training needs.
- Part of the standards and procedures for project planning describe how the work experience and training experience of allocated staff is to be displayed in the project plan.

20

SERVICING

20.1 INTRODUCTION

This part of the standard concerns what happens to the software product after it has been released to the customer:

> When servicing is specified in the contract, the supplier shall establish and maintain procedures for performing and verifying that servicing meets the specified requirements.

There are normally two aspects to servicing. The first is that of responding to reports from the customer which may pinpoint errors in the system that has been developed. The second is that of enhancing a system. The circumstances of a purchaser are never static: requirements will change with time and the purchaser will be keen that the software system that has been delivered follows these changes and is enhanced. These changes will vary from the purchase of hardware to changes in requirements such as those generated by a new financial law or new safety requirement. The important point to make about servicing—probably the most important point—is that the quality assurance used during servicing should be of the same level as that used for new development. All too often developers have excellent quality systems for development, but do not bother to apply them to the process of change during operation.

20.2 THE SERVICE CONTRACT

Where there is a requirement for servicing, the supplier and purchaser should agree on a service contract. This contract will contain information such as:

- The date from which the service agreement starts and the version of the software system which is extant on that date.

- Conditions about the speed of response of the supplier. For example, it may be stipulated in the contract that when the purchaser notifies the supplier about a possible fault the developer will respond within a specified time to inform the purchaser whether the notification involved a fault or was, for example, based on a misreading of the user manual.
- Details about how enhancements are to be dealt with. Normally enhancement requests will be charged by the supplier to the customer. Details need to be given about this process and the timing of when enhancements are added to the system. For example, the supplier and purchaser may agree that an enhancement is added to the next major version of the software or is implemented within a strict time period, for example when an enhancement due to a hardware change is required.
- The lines of communication between the purchaser and the supplier, i.e. who is allowed to communicate possible faults and enhancements and who is allowed to receive them.
- The documentation used to support the service function—documentation such as problem report forms.
- A specification of the evidence that should normally be provided by the supplier when reporting a fault. For example, the printout of a screen indicating a problem with a particular command.
- The period over which the service contract holds.
- The medium used to communicate new system versions. For example, the supplier and purchaser may agree that a small edit file is used to change the purchaser's version of the system and then recompile it.
- Any arbitration procedures if the supplier and purchaser disagree over whether a report of a fault is actually a fault or a misunderstanding of the system.

20.3 THE ORGANIZATION AND PLANNING OF THE SERVICE FUNCTION

The supplier should have a service function which is capable of communicating with the customer both by post and telephone and, in the future, by electronic mail. The service support function should act as a front-end to the configuration management system of the supplier. Normally the service function would carry out the following activities in response to the receipt of a possible error report:

1. A problem report is received and logged by service staff.
2. The supporting documentation sent by the customer to support the claim of an error is examined and a decision made as to whether the report actually represents an error. If it does not, then the customer is informed and the report is logged as a false alarm.
3. If the report is an error, then it is passed to the manager in charge of the servicing of the system who makes a preliminary estimate of the resources needed to rectify the error.
4. The manager then schedules the required staff to work on the process of eradicating the error.
5. Development staff eradicate the error and test the system to check whether the error has been fully corrected.

6. Development staff then check that the modifications that have been made have not affected those functions of the system which are not related to the fault discovered.

7. Development staff then modify the documentation that needs to be changed to reflect the modifications they have made. The nature of the error will dictate what documentation is modified. In the worst case it could mean modifying the requirements specification, system design, detailed designs of affected modules and the system test specification.

8. The version numbering of all affected documents is updated to reflect the change. If a two-level numbering system with a major version number and a minor version number is used, then the minor version number would be incremented by one.

9. The new version of the system is sent to the customer, together with any new test data which might be required to check out the new version of the system in its target environment.

For error eradication and minor functional enhancements the process described above is adequate, although for the latter some costing and charging of the change is required. For major enhancements a more project- oriented approach is required. In effect the software developer would set up a small project whose task is to implement the enhancements required by the user. This project would have its own project plan and quality plan and resemble any other project, apart from the fact that there will be extra tests, known as regression tests, which have the aim of checking that the new enhancements do not affect the existing functionality and performance of the system.

20.4 RELATION TO ISO 9000-3

The section of ISO 9000-3 which is relevant to this part of the standard is Section 5.10. The section is called *maintenance* rather than servicing. This book will assume that these two terms are synonymous. Section 5.10.1 specifies that all activities which are of a maintenance nature should be carried out in such a way that they respect the requirements for maintenance agreed between the supplier and the purchaser. This subsection also details the types of maintenance activities that are carried out on software. It identifies three activities: problem resolution; interface modification; and functional expansion or performance improvement. This book has collected the last two categories together and called the collection *enhancements*. The subsection makes the important point that not only program code should be considered as maintenance items but also data, specifications, purchaser's documents and supplier's documents. Subsection 5.10.2 specifies that a maintenance plan should be developed, the plan having been agreed between the supplier and the purchaser. This plan would contain items such as those detailed in Section 20.2 of this book.

Subsection 5.10.4 specifies that a service organization is often required by maintenance contracts and makes the point that this service organization should be capable of responding quickly and effectively to the unexpected occurrence of problems.

Subsection 5.10.5 makes the point that the same quality assurance procedures should be employed for maintenance as those employed in new development. It also provides an expanded description of the three main categories of changes that are detailed in Subsection 5.10.1 of ISO 9000-3.

Subsection 5.10.6 makes the important point that maintenance records should be kept during the period of maintenance. Typical records would include a summary of error reports received, the proportion of false alarms and some summary data which describes the severity of the errors.

Subsection 5.10.7 details what should happen about release procedures when an updated system is released to a purchaser. This includes procedures for applying code patches, the version numbering used in releases, the categories of release (minor or major) that are used by the supplier, how the purchaser will be told about future releases incorporating changes, methods used to check that a change has not adversely affected other functions of the system and data about which versions of the software have been released to which customers.

20.5 PROBLEMS

The problems which are encountered if this part of the standard is not adhered to are:

- Changes applied after release which are not adequately quality assured result in the gradual degradation of the quality of a system.
- Versions of a system are sent to the purchaser containing errors in functions which previously were correct.
- Supplier staff spend a large amount of time discovering which version of a software system a customer was previously sent.
- The wrong version of a system is sent to the purchaser after a modification or a series of modifications have been carried out.
- The supplier continually violates the provisions of a service contract because of an inadequate servicing plan.
- Functional enhancements are carried out under the guise of error eradication due to inadequate procedures for screening problem reports.
- Problem reports get lost or disappear because of inadequate communication mechanisms, or because the wrong person from the purchaser's side spoke to the wrong person from the supplier's side.

20.6 CHECKS

- A guideline exists which provides advice on the development of a service plan based on purchaser requirements.
- Procedures exist which deal with the processing of problem reports from the purchaser.
- Standards and procedures exist which specify how communication is to be organized between the supplier and the purchaser during servicing.
- Procedures exist which specify how data is to be collected during servicing.
- Standards exist which specify how the data collected during servicing is to be presented.
- Procedures exist which specify how staff carrying out the servicing function interact with the configuration management system adopted for servicing.

- Procedures exist which describe how a project is to be set up which implements enhancements to a system.
- Procedures exist which describe how enhancements to a system are to be costed.
- Procedures for regression testing exist for use during servicing.

$$21$$

STATISTICAL TECHNIQUES

21.1 INTRODUCTION

Many non-software engineering processes make extensive use of measurement. For example, manufacturers of items shaped from metals such as ball-bearings are able to predict variations from specified size by means of records generated from the past performance of machine tools. The software developer is not in such a fortunate position. Nevertheless, there are a number of measurements and statistical techniques that can be used to satisfy this part of the standard:

> Where appropriate, the supplier shall establish procedures for identifying adequate statistical techniques required for verifying the acceptability of process capability and product characteristics.

21.2 DEFECT MEASUREMENT

During the software project a developer will be validating a system against a number of documents; for example, a design will be validated against a requirements specification and individual modules will be tested against their specifications. These validation processes will give rise to defect data. The process of servicing will also give rise to defect data via error reports from customers. These two sources provide the software company with valuable information which can be used to evaluate a quality system, the developmental processes used by the supplier and the quality of individual systems which are released to the purchaser.

The supplier should have set up mechanisms whereby these defects are documented in such a way that summary data can be extracted easily. For example, for released software, the staff who are responsible for servicing should, as a minimum, keep statistics of the number, extent and severity of the errors notified by purchasers. It is important, however, to realise that quite a few of these 'errors' are often generated by the purchaser's staff misunderstanding the user manual, or by the purchaser attempting to get a requirements change implemented at little or no cost. Therefore some screening is needed before errors are transformed into statistics. It is also important that some statistics are kept on the reasons for errors. Now, it is clearly impractical for a company to carry out a post-mortem on each and every error. Nevertheless, it is important that quite a high proportion of errors are explained by reference to deficiencies in either the quality system or the developmental processes employed. This is particularly important for errors which are categorized as very serious and which require substantial reworking in order to eradicate them.

Tips and techniques 28

One of the most useful metrics to employ on a third-generation software project is that of the fan-out of a module. This is defined as the number of modules that a module calls in order to carry out its function. The larger the fan-out the more problems the module will give. In general those modules which have a larger fan-out are attempting to do more work than they should. Often such modules are multi-functional in that they carry out function $f1$, function $f2$ and so on, when in a good system architecture each module should carry out only *one* function. Such modules give major problems during programming, integration, system testing and acceptance testing. However, the activity which they affect most adversely is maintenance. It is a good idea to restrict the fan-out of modules to no more than a relatively small number. I would suggest five.

21.3 PROJECT MONITORING STATISTICS

At the beginning of a software project a project manager will have identified all the tasks which make up a project, have allocated resources to them and estimated the amount of time that each task will take. One use for this information is for project estimating.

During a project, staff will be reporting on task completion and will be providing information such as the date on which the task was completed and how much resource has been expended on the task. This information can be processed and provide the project manager with important statistics such as: the amount of project resource expended to date; the extent to which the project resource expenditure matches predicted resource expenditure; the extent to which the project progress matches predicted time progress; slippage in terms of resources; and slippage in terms of time.

21.4 SOFTWARE METRICS

An increasingly important area of research which is now bearing fruit on real software projects is that of software measurement. Software metrics are measurements which can be extracted from a product of a software project such as a system design. A metric measures some aspects of a product which can, theoretically, be used to control some quality factor. For example, the depth of nesting of control structures in a third-generation language module contributes to the readability of the module: a high depth of nesting results in a module that is difficult to read and hence difficult to modify during maintenance.

Research on measurement is not sufficiently advanced that companies are able to predict factors such as time to debug a module and time to understand a design from metric data. However, it is sufficiently advanced to use metrics as a quality control, for example by insisting that developmental staff do not exceed some metric threshold in the items that they produce. Simple metrics which could be used in a software project include the number of lines of code in a module and the complexity of Boolean conditions in a program expressed in terms of the maximum number of specific Boolean operators and the number of test cases used to check out a function in a requirements specification.

21.5 RELATION TO ISO 9000-3

Section 6.4 of ISO 9000-3 describes two types of measurements: product measurements and process measurements. From the descriptions of these measurements there seems to be some overlap. However, in general, product measurement seems to refer to defect data. This part of ISO 9000-3 urges developers to use product metrics in order to gain information about when remedial action is to be taken and to establish improvement goals in terms of measures such as the level and number of defects reported.

ISO 9000-3 also urges the use of process metrics. These are measures taken from software processes such as programming, in order to track project progress and the effectiveness of the quality plan in reducing the number of errors.

21.6 PROBLEMS

The problems which are encountered if this part of the standard is not adhered to are:

- Inadequate feedback from projects on important statistics such as the degree of slippage of a project.
- Inadequate feedback on the quality of the delivered product. This leads to a lack of confidence in the supplier by the purchaser.
- A valuable source of data which could be used for quality system improvement is lost.

21.7 CHECKS

- A guideline exists which provides advice on the collection of error statistics.
- Standards and procedures exist for the gathering and presentation of error statistics for errors which are generated during development.
- Standards and procedures exist for the gathering and presentation of error statistics for errors which are notified to the developer after delivery.

- As part of the project planning standards and procedures a project manager is instructed to include information about task timing and task resourcing in the project plan.
- Standards exist for the documentation generated when a task has been completed.
- Procedures exist which ask staff to fill in task completion documentation when a task has been completed.
- Guidelines exist which detail the possible uses of well-tried product metrics.

INDEX